OUTDOOR STONEWORK

OUTDOOR STONEWORK

16 easy-to-build projects for your yard and garden

A L A N & G I L L B R I D G E W A T E R

STOREY

The mission of Storey Publishing is to serve our customers by publishing practical information that encourages personal independance in harmony with the environment.

North American edition published in 2001 by Storey Books,
210 MASS MoCA Way, North Adams, MA 01247.

First published in 2001 by New Holland Publishers (UK) Ltd
London • Cape Town • Sydney • Auckland

Editorial Direction: Rosemary Wilkinson
Project Editor: Kate Latham
Production: Caroline Hansell

Designed and created for New Holland by AG&G BOOKS
Design: Glyn Bridgewater
Illustrators: Alan and Gill Bridgewater
Project design: Alan and Gill Bridgewater
Photography: Ian Parsons
Editor: Fiona Corbridge
Stonework: Alan and Gill Bridgewater

Reproduction by Colour Symphony, Singapore
Printed and bound in Malaysia by Times Offset (M) Sdn. Bhd.

Storey Books are available for special premium and promotional uses and for customized editions. For further information, please call Storey's Custom Publishing Department at 1-800-793-9396.

Library of Congress Cataloging-in-Publication Data

Bridgewater, Alan.
  Outdoor stonework: 16 easy-to-build projects for your yard and garden /
Alan & Gill Bridgewater.
    p. cm.
  Includes index.
  ISBN 1-58017-333-0 (pbk.)
    1. Garden structures--Design and construction--Amateurs' manuals. 2.
Stonemasonry--Amateurs' manuals. 3. Garden construction--Amateurs' manuals. 4.
Decoration and ornament, Architectural--Amateurs' manuals. I. Bridgewater, Gill. II.
Title.

TH4961 .B58 2000
624.1'832--dc21
                                          00-056296

Contents

Introduction 6

Part 1: Techniques 8

Part 2: Projects 32

Introduction

When we first saw the stone walls that formed the garden boundary of our Cornish quayside cottage, we were amazed. They were beautiful! Ranging in height from a meter to well over three meters, the walls were massively thick and built from course upon course of uncut limestone. And so it was with all the walls in the village. We were brought to a standstill not only by the sheer size of the structures, but also by their physical presence and the fact that every single stone was set in place without mortar.

From then on, we were hooked. We began to scour the countryside for examples of interesting stonework. Over the next few years, we saw stone steps that disappeared into the sea, massive stonework railway arches built by Isambard Kingdom Brunel, tin mine towers, stone cellars, and so on. After years of looking and touching, exploring and drawing, we wanted to have a go at stonework ourselves. We began to search for some good "how-to" books, but soon discovered that although there were plenty of books that described stone structures, there was nothing much that actually told you how to mix the mortar and set one stone upon another. We came to the conclusion that if we wanted to do

stonework, we simply had to get on with it. As a result, we have worked on all manner of garden stonework projects – everything from walls and pillars, paths and rockeries, through to Japanese gardens and gateposts – and enjoyed it immensely.

Stonework is an amazingly vigorous and dynamic craft. The forms are large and bold, the techniques are adventurous and expressive, and the end results are truly monumental and last forever. We invite you to roll up your sleeves, take up the challenge, and build something that you will be very proud of!

Alan & Gill

Part I: Techniques

Designing and planning

The secret of building a successful stonework feature lies in the detail. It does not matter whether you are young or old; what is more important is enthusiasm and a willingness to spend time designing and planning the whole operation – from choosing the individual stones to organizing the delivery, mixing the mortar, and cleaning your tools. Stonework will enhance any garden, whether it is large or small.

FIRST CONSIDERATIONS

- Do you live in an area where the predominant building material is stone? Are there stone quarries within a radius of 30 miles (20 kilometers)?
- If most of the houses near you are built from brick and wood (therefore the chances are that there are no stone quarries in your area), are there any other sources of supply, such as builder's merchants or architectural salvage companies?
- Will local companies deliver small quantities of mixed stone?
- Is there adequate access to your garden – a road clear of traffic, a wide gateway, and a good driveway?
- If the stone is unloaded in your driveway, or at your gate, will it cause any problems of access for you or your car? Will it damage the surface of the driveway? Will it pose a danger to children or passersby?
- How are you going to move the stone from the gate to the site? Are you going to move it yourself with a wheelbarrow and a hand truck? Or are you going to ask friends to help, then move it with the aid of levers and rollers?
- Is your garden reasonably level, with paths wide enough for a wheelbarrow? Or does it have a lot of lawn and few pathways – if so, how will you move the materials?

Choosing a suitable project

When you have found satisfactory solutions to obtaining the stone and have worked out how and when it is going to be delivered, you can start to consider the ergonomics of the projects in the context of your specific needs: This boils down to working out how you are going to move the stone around the garden. In most instances, we have specifically designed the projects so that they are made from small, easy-to-lift stones (albeit the sum total weight of all the stones might be considerable), but one or two of the projects do use single, monolithic stones. For example, if you have chosen to make the Pedestal Table (page 120), you have to work out how you are going to lift the table slab into position. There are a couple of ways to deal with it: You can build the pedestal before you take delivery of the table slab, then ask the stone supplier to lift the slab straight into position, or you can call on your friends and family to help you. The only thing you mustn't do is back down from building the project!

Planning the project

Whoever said that stonework is made up in equal parts of inspiration, perspiration, and planning was right. Miscalculations can result in many hours of wasted time and effort. For example, when we failed to remember that a 3-ton delivery of gravel was arriving one day, it was simply tipped in our gateway. It was a good thing the sun was shining, because we spent about 18 hours moving it in a wheelbarrow – just so we could use the car!

Plan your projects in as much detail as possible. It makes sense to schedule the building for a time of year when the weather is likely to be reasonable so that the concrete will dry quickly and easily and does not need to be protected from frost. When you have taken delivery of the sand, cement, and stone, you need to consider the finer points of the operation. Is the structure going to get in the way of other activities? Is the ground so boggy, bumpy, or rocky that you need to rethink the foundation? Are you building over an existing underground electricity cable? Is the structure going to cause water to collect? Are all the comings and goings with wheelbarrows and water going to damage the lawn? Are neighbors going to object? And so on. When all these questions have been answered, move all the materials to the site and cover them so that they are shielded from the weather.

Buying the right tools and materials

When you are starting to do stonework, buy yourself a basic, inexpensive tool kit appropriate for the project that you intend to make. But in the long run, expensive, high-quality tools are the best option because they will last for years.

It is sensible for beginners to buy their materials one bag at a time; however, it is far cheaper to order sand, gravel, cement, and rock in bulk. For example, twenty 80-pound (50 kg) bags of gravel purchased one at a time from the local builder's merchant cost the same as a 4-ton truckload of loose gravel ordered from a quarry. Much the same goes for all the other materials. So, buy materials in bulk if possible to cut costs to the minimum.

The general rule of thumb is the more you want to buy, the lower the cost per unit, and most specialist suppliers are more than happy to haggle over the price. So, phone up at least three suppliers, specify your needs, and see who gives you the lowest quote. Then ask the other two suppliers if they want to better that price. Once you have agreed to the price over the phone, ask the supplier to confirm your order in writing, setting out the product quantities, the total cost, and the delivery date and time.

STONEWORK DESIGNS FOR THE GARDEN

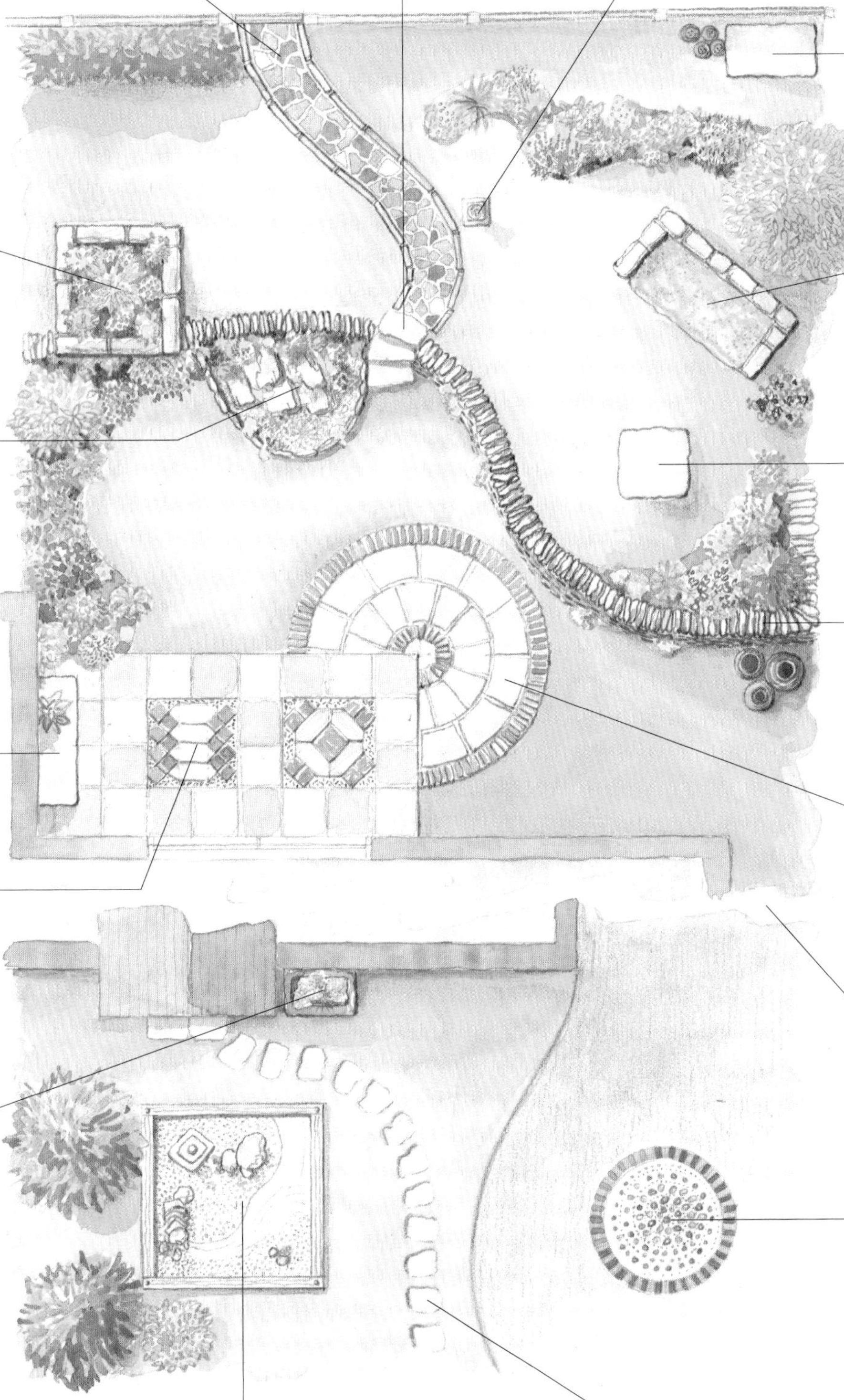

Multicolored crazy paving
A colorful and creative way to build a winding path

Flagstone steps
Useful for getting up and down sloping earth banks and terraces

Sundial
Positioned away from trees so that it is in full sunshine most of the day

Raised bed
An attractive feature for displaying your favorite flowers – and making weeding much easier

Flagstone potting table
Set in a sheltered area against a wall

Natural outcrop rock garden
Built against a wall or terrace

Camomile bench
Placed in a spot with a good view of the garden

Cantilevered seat-shelf
Built against a thick, strong wall. Useful for container plants or just for sitting on

Pedestal table
Set on a level area of lawn with space around it for chairs

Dry-stone retaining wall
Can be used to support a rock garden or terrace

Tessellated paving
Located near to the house, forming a convenient patio area

Paved circle
Shown here as three-quarters of a circle extending from the tessellated paving

Alpine hypertufa trough
Placed in a sheltered position near to the house and facing the morning sun

White strip represents position of house

Cobble spiral
This design improves a bland driveway

ABOVE **This design demonstrates how the projects in this book might be used to landscape and furnish your garden with attractive stonework features.**

Tranquil Japanese garden
Placed in a quiet and secluded area of the garden

Stepping-stone path
Positioned to reduce wear and tear on the lawn – a quick and nonintrusive solution

Tools

The secret of tackling the projects successfully is using the correct tools for the job. A top-quality tool will make a huge difference to the ease with which a task can be accomplished. It is altogether more comfortable to hold, longer lasting, and ensures that tasks are completed in as short a time as possible.

TOOLS FOR HANDLING STONE

Gloves

Bucket

Hand truck

Wheelbarrow

Protecting your feet and hands

Wear solid leather workboots, preferably with reinforced steel toecaps, to prevent your feet from getting squashed by a stray dropped stone, and work gloves to save your hands from getting cut, abraded, and otherwise damaged. The gloves might take a while to get used to, but they will protect your hands from the relentless wear and tear that is involved in working with a hammer and chisel, lifting stones, and mixing sand and cement.

Making the work easier

Of all the tools you can buy, it is the wheelbarrow, hand truck and bucket that make life easier when tackling stonework. By the time you get to the end of a project you will have formed a deep and loving relationship with both your wheelbarrow and hand truck! A good wheelbarrow will save your back from a huge amount of stress and strain. If you buy one with a large inflated rubber tire and a tip-stop bar that protrudes in front, you will be able to bounce your way up steps and over rocks, and just as easily be

able to stop and tip out the load from the barrow. The wheelbarrow is used primarily for transporting wet and dry granular materials such as loose earth, sand, gravel, and concrete.

A hand truck is used for moving single, heavy items such as bags of cement, flagstones, or large chunks of stone. It works on the lever principle, enabling you to lift and move weights that would otherwise be completely unmanageable. To use it, you nudge the platform under the item to be moved, pull back on the handles so that the weight is sitting over the wheels (over the fulcrum), then go on your way. A good, strong hand truck will, depending upon the mass of the object, allow you to move anything up to 300–400 pounds (150–200 kg) in weight with ease.

Finally, you need three or four plastic buckets. Don't bother about buying good-quality items, because buckets are more or less disposable – just buy the cheapest that you can find and use them until they fall apart. Some suppliers will cut the price if you purchase in multiples. Buckets are used for a variety of tasks, including transporting water for mixing into mortar and concrete.

TOOLS FOR MEASURING AND MARKING

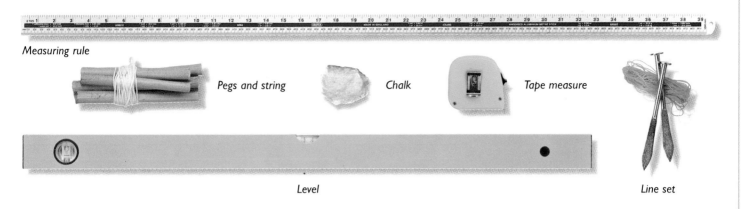

Measuring rule

Pegs and string *Chalk* *Tape measure*

Level *Line set*

Measuring

Ideally, you need two measuring tools – a flexible tape measure for setting out the site plan and a rule for measuring individual rocks and blocks within the project. Make sure that both tools are marked out in metric and English so that you can deal with products that are described in either system. If possible, buy a waterproof, fiberglass tape measure, as this will stand up better to the damp and dirt involved in stoneworking.

Marking out

The main tools are pegs and string for setting out the foundation on the ground, chalk for drawing a plan on a concrete base, and a level for checking the horizontal and vertical levels within the structure. Buy one with a strong aluminium body. You may also wish to use a line set for guiding the courses of stone and esti-mating the course heights. The pegs are stuck into the ground (or a course), and the line stretched between them.

TOOLS FOR PREPARING A SITE

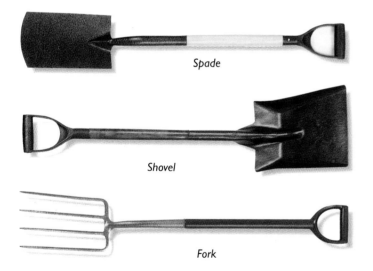

Spade

Shovel

Fork

Sledgehammer

Lawn rake

Garden rake

Removing sod and digging earth

A spade is used to prepare the site. Having marked out the size of the foundation, take the spade, cut down through the thickness of the sod, and slice it into easy-to-manage squares. Scoop it straight into the wheelbarrow and remove it from the site. Finally, dig out the earth to the required depth and clean out to a flat base.

Compacting hardcore and raking

A sledgehammer will make short work of compacting hardcore. The smaller the stones, the easier it is to compact – builder's rubble requires a lot of effort, while crushed stone more or less puts itself into place. The procedure is simple: spread a thin layer over the foundation area and pound it into place, walking back-ward and forward over it from time to time.

The tool used for raking depends upon the material in ques-tion. It is best to use a fork for moving and breaking up clumps of earth, a garden rake for spreading gravel, and a lawn rake for spreading sand and for tidying up.

Mixing cement and moving gravel

The simplest way of mixing cement and moving gravel is to use a carefully chosen, good-quality shovel. Wash the shovel after mixing cement. Never try shoveling with a spade or digging with a shovel – both exercises are a backbreaking waste of time!

TOOLS FOR SHAPING STONE

Mason's hammer

Angle grinder

Cold chisel

Bolster chisel

Drill hammer

Breaking stone

One of the most direct ways of shaping or truing up stone (meaning to tap off a corner or shape an edge) is to use a mason's hammer, sometimes known as a brick hammer. The hammer is used on its own, without a chisel of any description. Cradle the stone (in your hand, on soft ground, or on a pad) and strike it repeatedly, working in a line. Flip it over and repeat the procedure on the other side until the waste piece falls away.

To trim an edge back to a drawn line, the mason's hammer can again be used alone. Hold the stone with the edge to be worked nearest to you, then hit it with a series of rapid pecks so that the waste falls away as chips. If you find that you enjoy working with stone and decide that you are going to try lots of the projects, it would be a good idea to get yourself a good-quality leather apron as added protection from flying slivers of stone.

Cutting stone

While breaking stone with a mason's hammer is relatively approximate, cutting stone is a more accurate procedure that involves using a drill hammer with a bolster chisel or a cold chisel.

The bolster chisel is used for hefty tasks such as chopping a stone in half. To cut a stone down the run of the grain – in much the same way as splitting a log – you simply set the chisel on the end grain and work backward and forward until you see the stone begin to fracture. You then work away at a crack until the stone splits into two pieces. To break a large stone across the run of the grain – like cutting a long log into two lengths – draw a line with chalk and hit it with the drill hammer and bolster chisel. Repeatedly work around all the faces until the stone falls into two.

A cold chisel is appropriate for more delicate tasks, such as trimming an edge, or other fine adjustments.

Sawing stone

In the context of this book, sawing stone involves using an electric angle grinder to cut flagstone slabs. The grinder is first fitted with a stone-cutting disk, as described by the manufacturer. You must wear a dust mask, a pair of goggles, gloves, and durable work-boots. The grinder is connected up to an 110 volt power supply. The disk is placed on the drawn line and the tool is run forward to make the cut. As the angle grinder creates an enormous amount of dust, it is best to work outside, setting the stone down flat on the grass and holding it with your foot (keeping it well away from the line of cut). It does not matter if the disk slips off at the end of the line, because it simply cuts into the grass and no damage is done. If you feel at all unhappy about the prospect of using an angle grinder, ask a knowledgeable friend to show you how to do it. Never use a grinder if you are tired or in any way under stress.

CAUTION

It is vital to wear goggles for all stone-breaking and cutting operations, to protect your eyes from dust, chips of stone and fragments of metal. Wear a dust-mask when using the angle grinder.

TOOLS FOR CONCRETE AND MORTAR

Pointing trowel

Mortar float

Bricklayer's trowel

Spreading concrete and mortar

If you want to achieve a smooth finish once the concrete or mortar has been tipped into place, you have to use a mortar float or plasterer's trowel. Made from steel, wood, or plastic, the float is used with an even, side-to-side smoothing action – in much the same way as you use a bricklayer's trowel. If you want the water to rise to the surface (to create an ultrasmooth finish), use a steel float, otherwise one made from plastic or wood will suffice. Always clean the float under running water after use, especially on the underside and around the handle.

Handling mortar

The bricklayer's trowel is designed for transferring large slaps of mortar. The pointing trowel is shaped for pointing and for raking out some of the mortar from between the courses for decorative effect. Many beginners find it easier to use the smaller pointing trowel for both tasks. Use the tool that you feel comfortable with and change over if and when you feel the need. Many people find that although the large trowel certainly gets the mortar shifted quickly, its weight puts a strain on the wrist. Make sure that your chosen trowel has a well-shaped handle that feels good to hold.

TOOLS FOR FINISHING A PROJECT

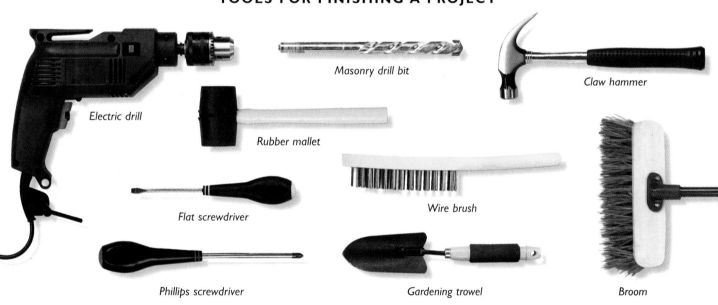

Masonry drill bit

Claw hammer

Electric drill

Rubber mallet

Wire brush

Flat screwdriver

Phillips screwdriver

Gardening trowel

Broom

Holes and fixings

Stonework also involves drilling holes, banging in nails, and driving in screws. It is best to use an electric drill in conjunction with a masonry drill bit for boring holes into rock, a carpenter's claw hammer for nailing foundation frames, and both flat and Phillips screwdrivers for pushing home the screws. If a giant-size electric drill is required, rent it by the day.

Leveling and cleaning

You may find a rubber mallet useful for nudging individual stones into place. A wire brush is excellent for cleaning stray blobs of mortar from the stone when the mortaring process is finished. At the end of a long day's work, a good, stiff-bristled broom makes it much easier to get through the tedious task of tidying up. Wash the broom after use to remove grit and grime from the head and handle, and store it with the head uppermost so the bristles have a chance to dry out.

Planting

A gardening trowel is needed for planting a selection of plants in projects such as the Natural Outcrop Rock Garden (page 42) and the Raised Bed (page 52). It is also a handy little tool for scooping up small amounts of sand and cement. Buy a couple of them and use them for the various tasks.

Materials

We are not concerned about the geological makeup of the various materials – apart from identification, it does not contribute anything to the projects to know whether a rock is igneous or metamorphic. We have concentrated on the common names and the working characteristics of the rocks.

NATURAL STONE

York stone

Flagstone

Rockery stone

Limestone

Pink limestone

Wall limestone

Reclaimed slate

Cobbles

Paddle stone

Napped flint

Roof slate

Limestone

Limestone was once very popular as a building stone because it is easy to shape, in any direction, to make steps, slabs, and blocks. However, there are now so many reconstituted stone look-alike "limestone" blocks on the market that the genuine item has fallen from favor. While it is prohibitively expensive to use new sawn and faced limestone, salvaged architectural limestone is reasonably priced. When we needed cut blocks of white stone to make the Japanese lantern for the Tranquil Japanese Garden (page 82), we found salvaged limestone to be by far the best option because it had the most attractive appearance.

Always identify the direction of the grain prior to laying the blocks, making sure that the layers within the grain sit horizontally rather than vertically. If you are not sure which way the grain runs, look very closely at the salvaged stone to see how the various faces were arranged in their previous setting, then simply copy the arrangement in your project.

Sandstone

Sandstone and limestone are both formed by deposition – meaning that the stone is created from layers of material put under enormous pressure. Limestone is made up of organic remains such as shell and bones, and sandstone is made of particles of quartz or sand. Sandstone ranges in color from pinky red and brown to black, green, and blue-grey. Some stones are so hard that they ring when struck, while others are so soft and crumbly that they can be broken like dry biscuits. Depending upon the variety, sandstone is good for dry-stone walling, stepping-stones, and flagstones. Always avoid stone that flakes when touched, as it is likely to have been damaged by frost.

Slate

The geological formation of slate is the result of the heating of clay deposits under pressure. Slate is characterized by its blue, black, or green color and smooth, shiny surface. It can be split into thin sheets, which are mainly used for roofing.

In this book, slate is used in the form of small packs of "paddle" stone sold by quarries and as broken roof stone sold by architectural salvage companies. While slate does not easily blend in with limestone and sandstone, so it cannot be used in large lumps in equal partnership, small pieces make an effective color contrast. For example, the Flagstone Potting Table (page 108) uses thin layers of slate with deeply raked joints to contrast with the rather severe blocks of limestone. Be aware, when you are

choosing your stone, that the terms "slate" and "roofing stone" are commonly interchanged and used to describe all manner of stone types that can be broken into thin sheets.

Granite

While there is no denying that granite is immensely strong and attractive in both color and texture – ranging from dark green-blue through to a pinkish grey – it is also so hard that it is almost impossible to work. Certainly you can just about make headway with a grinder, and sometimes you can be lucky with a hammer and bolster chisel, but mostly it is too difficult to cut. If you really want to use granite, search out pieces in the stoneyard that suit your needs as they stand. For example, you could use salvaged road blocks and kerbstones to build the lantern in the Tranquil Japanese Garden (page 82), pavers to edge the Paved Circle (page 70), massive pieces of quarry stone as feature stones in the Natural Outcrop Rock Garden (page 42), or even large salvaged field posts as guardians or sentinels. Be very wary about obtaining pieces of granite that are bigger than you need, because they are usually so impossible to work that the task is not worth the wear and tear on your tools. One of the best ways of using granite is in its crushed state, as a decorative spread.

RECONSTITUTED STONE

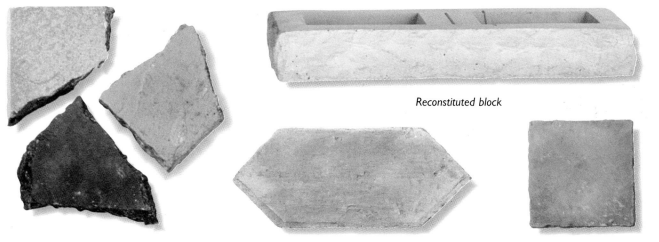

Reconstituted block

Crazy paving　　　　*Reconstituted tessellating tile*　　　　*Reconstituted slab*

Reconstituted blocks

Reconstituted stone blocks are concrete blocks – sometimes made with an aggregate containing the stone that they seek to imitate – that are made to look like natural stone. There are double-sided blocks that imitate rough-tooled limestone, blocks that look like fieldstone, blocks that resemble sawn limestone, and so on. In many instances, you can cut costs by collecting the blocks direct from the manufacturer.

You may wish to substitute reconstituted blocks in the projects to save money, but they are usually not as beautiful as the real thing. The best way to regard them is as a little taster that will lead you into the more exciting adventure of using natural stone.

Reconstituted slabs

While reconstituted blocks can look quite crude, reconstituted slabs, on the other hand, are a great idea. Made in much the same way as the blocks, often with an aggregate containing the stone that they are masquerading as, many reconstituted slabs are so convincing that at first sight they cannot be distinguished from the real thing. Such slabs come in all sorts of shapes, sizes, colors, and textures: tessellating shapes that look like red quarry tiles, sand-stone paving slabs, on-edge stone and brick slabs, limestone and sandstone flagstones, and many other forms and designs. If you want to cut costs, they can be substituted when a project calls for thin layers of stone. Pick slabs that are described as "color-fast".

CHIPS, GRAVEL, CEMENT, AND LIME

Limestone chips

Smooth gravel

Pink gravel

Medium gravel

Pea gravel

Oyster shell

Sharp sand

Sand and gravel

Soft sand

Cement

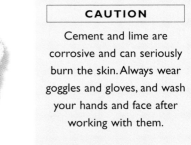

Lime

> **CAUTION**
>
> Cement and lime are corrosive and can seriously burn the skin. Always wear goggles and gloves, and wash your hands and face after working with them.

Soft sand

Soft sand, sometimes called builder's sand, is used for making smooth-textured mortar. Sold by the bag or truckload, the color and texture of the soft sand available will usually relate to the color of the stone in your area. If you are building with local stone, it is best to use local soft sand. However, builder's suppliers purchase some sand from distant quarries, so you do have to check the color of your intended purchase to make sure it is suitable. If you are looking for good color and low cost, your best option is to order your sand in bulk from a local pit.

Always make sure that the sand has been well washed and is free from salt and particles of clay. Salt damages mortar and concrete. If the sand smells rank or contains animal or vegetable matter or looks in any way contaminated, go to another supplier.

Sharp sand

Sharp sand is nearly always used for making concrete and is also added to soft sand to make a coarse, bulky mortar. In terms of color and cost, much the same can be said for sharp sand as for soft. Whether the sand comes from a pit, quarry, or river or is a mixture of naturally occurring sand and crushed stone, it is vital that it is free from clay, loam, and organic matter.

Check it if you have any doubts: Clean sand will not stain your fingers, and if you put it in a glass of water, shake it up, and leave it to stand, you should end up with just a thin film of silt on top of the sand, and clear water. If there is a layer of scum floating on the water and a salty smell – a bit like a beach at low tide – then the chances are that it is unwashed sea sand, which is totally unsuitable for making mortar and concrete.

Cement

Cement powder – sold in 94-pound (25 kg and 50 kg) bags and described generically as "Portland cement" – is one of the chief ingredients of mortar and concrete. Though it is undoubtedly true to say that you can save money by ordering a large number of 94-pound bags, this is the one instance where it is much better to buy just enough for the job in hand. Not only are 94-pound bags difficult to handle, but they are also flimsy and liable to tear, the cement powder is susceptible to moisture, and loose powder is highly corrosive and very bad for the skin, eyes, and lungs.

Lime

Lime is used together with cement and sand to make mortar. Though a "cement mortar" can be made without lime (undoubtedly harder and stronger than lime and cement mortar), it is also so hard that it stains the stone and pulls it apart. As with cement powder, it is best to order lime in small quantities and to store it in a dry place. Lime is highly corrosive, to the extent that you should wear goggles and a mask when mixing, and gloves for general handling. If you are mixing on a windy day, when the lime is blowing about, wash your face and hands afterward.

Aggregates

Concrete consists of Portland cement and a mixture of sand and stone known as an aggregate. The shape and size of the particles of sand and stone within the aggregate decide the character of the concrete – meaning its strength, hardness, durability, and porosity.

Commonly, aggregate is made up from graded sand, broken stone, and various types of crushed and graded gravel. For the projects in this book, choose an average mix made from small-sized gravel and sand. If you want to make a very coarse concrete for a thin leveling slab, you can bulk up your mix by adding a small amount of crushed brick or broken stone – just break it up with a hammer, dampen it, and add it to the mix.

Gravel, limestone chips, or oyster shell may also be laid down as a decorative surface. Choose a fine gravel such as pea gravel for a delicate appearance; limestone chips provide a chunkier effect. Gravel color depends on the stone it is made from.

OTHER MATERIALS

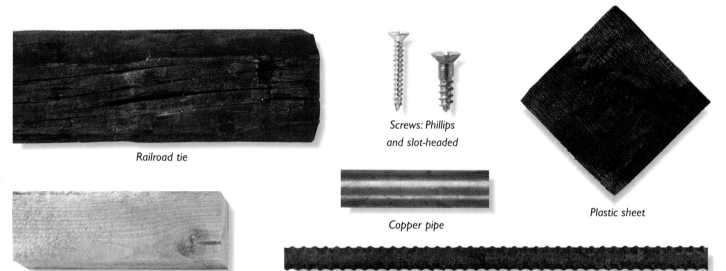

Railroad tie

Screws: Phillips and slot-headed

Copper pipe

Plastic sheet

Rough-sawn pine section

Iron reinforcing bar

Wood and fixings

Foundation frames should be made from rough-sawn softwood, as sold by most garden centers. Do not worry too much about the quality of the wood or the length of time it has been seasoned – other than to see that it is reasonably strong along its length. To fix these temporary frames, you can use a mixture of screws and nails, or whatever is handy. It's a good idea to use high-quality, pressure-treated wood to make the frame for the Tranquil Japanese Garden (page 82).

The lengths of railroad tie used under the Alpine Hypertufa Trough (page 62) and for bending the copper pipe in the Cantilevered Seat-Shelf (page 96) can be obtained as small scraps. Avoid railroad ties that ooze tar or creosote – they will ruin the tools and stain your hands and clothes.

Metal and plastics

The iron bar and copper pipe used for the Cantilevered Seat-Shelf (page 96) can be obtained from a builder's merchant as inexpensive scraps. The iron bar is sold as reinforcement bar, or "rebar," while the copper tube is used for plumbing. The plastic sheet used under the Tranquil Japanese Garden (page 82) is available from builder's merchants, plastics suppliers, or garden centers.

If you are eager to cut down on costs, visit the nearest building site and see if the site manager can spare you any scraps. If you are successful in your quest, before you take your haul away it's a good idea to ask the site manager to sign a note to the effect that the materials have been given to you, just in case you are questioned by the site security guards. Scrap metal merchants may also be willing to let you have small items free of charge.

Mixing mortar and concrete

Stonework involves the frequent mixing of mortar (for laying stone) and concrete (for foundations). If you can achieve a mix with a good texture, color, and working consistency, the construction process will go smoothly. Follow the old adage that says, "Mixing a little, not a lot, gets the job done in half the time".

MIXING A SMALL AMOUNT OF MORTAR IN A WHEELBARROW

Mixing procedure

1 Use a shovel to carefully measure the dry ingredients into the wheelbarrow – first the sand, then the Portland cement and the lime. Continue until the barrow is about half full. Turn the ingredients over several times until they are thoroughly mixed.
2 Pour about one-third of a bucket of water into one end of the wheelbarrow, then drag small amounts of the dry mix into the water. Repeat the process until all the water has been soaked up by the dry mix.
3 Turn over the whole heap several times, all the while adding small amounts of water, until you can chop it into clean, wet slices.

Mixing
Drag the dry mix into the water

MIXING A COARSE LIME AND CEMENT MORTAR

This mortar is made up of a 50/50 mixture of soft sand and sharp sand, Portland cement and lime. Because it is coarse, it is good for filling large gaps and wide courses. Measure the dry ingredients onto a board with a shovel – first the sand, then the cement and lime. Mix it up, dig a hole in the center, and pour in about half a bucket of water. Work around the heap, dragging small amounts of the dry mix into the water. If the water threatens to break over the rim, swiftly pull in more of the dry mix to stem the flow. When the water has been soaked up, add more until the mortar is the correct consistency. The finished mixture should form crisp, firm slices that stand up under their own weight without crumbling.

ABOVE It is often convenient to use a wheelbarrow for mixing mortar – bear in mind that you will need to give it a good cleaning afterward.

MORTAR AND CONCRETE MIXES

Smooth lime and cement mortar
Lime and cement mortar, suitable for fine- to medium-course stonework, is made up from 2 parts Portland cement, 1 part lime, and 9 parts soft sand. The sand should be chosen to complement the color of the stone.

Coarse lime and cement mortar
A coarse lime and cement mortar, appropriate for bulking up wide courses, can be constructed from 2 parts cement, 1 part lime, 4 parts soft sand, and 4 parts sharp sand. The proportion of sharp sand to soft sand should be modified to suit the texture of your chosen stone.

Concrete for foundations
A good, general-purpose concrete, suitable for small footings and foundations, is made of 1 part Portland cement, 2 parts sharp sand, and 3 parts aggregate. (The aggregate is made from gravel graded to pass through a 25-millimeter sieve.)

MIXING CONCRETE FOR FOUNDATION FOOTINGS

A concrete suitable for foundations contains cement, sharp sand, and aggregate. With a shovel, measure the sand and the Portland cement onto the board. Turn over the mixture thoroughly until it is well blended. Dig a hole in the center of the mound, pour in about half a bucket of water, then gradually drag the dry mix into the water. Continue until you achieve a wet, sloppy mixture. Finally, measure in the aggregate. Continue turning it over and adding small amounts of water until a shovelful of the mixture holds its shape when it is formed into a ridge.

Moving stone

Even though we live in an age of cranes and hoists, you will almost certainly have to physically move the stone by hand from the driveway, where it has been delivered, to the site in the garden. This section shows you how to do it with ease. But if you suspect that a stone is too heavy, ask a friend to help rather than risking injury.

MOVING HEAVY SLABS

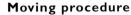

Moving the slab
Rock the slab onto one corner and pivot it around

Use rough board to protect your lawn

Moving procedure

1 Slabs weigh about 300–400 pounds (150–200 kg), so ask a friend to help you. First, use a sledgehammer to bang a couple of wooden wedges under one edge of the slab to lift it about 3 inches (70 mm) off the ground. Put two boards on the ground in the spot where the slab will be. Leave a small gap between them.

2 Together, grip the jacked-up edge of the stone (the stronger person being ready to push, and the other person ready to pull and steady). Heave the stone upright until it is standing on edge.

3 Rock the slab onto one of the bottom corners and pivot it so that the raised corner is pointing in the direction of the site. Lower this corner, then swing the other corner around, "walking" the slab across the garden. Keep stopping to rest along the way.

4 When you have reached the new location, lower the stone onto the boards (these maintain a gap between the stone and the ground, preventing your hands from getting trapped). Lift an edge and ease the boards out.

MOVING HEAVY ROCKERY STONES

Moving procedure

1 Having asked a friend to help, take a solid metal wheelbarrow (one with a large pneumatic tire) and wheel it up to the stone. Lie it on its side with one edge alongside the stone.

2 Place a pad of old carpet between the stone and the wheelbarrow, then maneuver the stone into the wheelbarrow. One of you eases the stone and the other holds the wheelbarrow.

3 When the stone is in the wheelbarrow, push and pull the wheelbarrow into an upright position, working together. Ease the stone to lie over the wheel. Always be ready to steady the wheelbarrow during its journey.

RIGHT Roll heavy stones, if possible, rather than lifting them. To protect your back when you have to lift a heavy weight, keep your knees bent, with your spine upright, and your weight balanced over your feet.

The helper pulls the wheelbarrow upright

Roll the stone into the wheelbarrow — avoid lifting it

Cutting stone

In many ways, the art and craft of good stonework is concerned with fitting and using stone as you find it. But when there is no option other than to make a cut, the main part of the challenge is getting it right. Today, much cutting is done with an electric angle grinder, but traditional chisels are still required for some tasks.

CUTTING STONE USING AN ANGLE GRINDER

Choosing the correct angle grinder

Angle grinders are deceptively easy to use, but it is important to choose the correct grinder for your needs. While it is generally easier to use a heavy-duty 9-inch-diameter (230 mm) grinder than it is to use a lightweight 4½-inch-diameter (115 mm) model, most beginners are not going to get much use out of a large grinder. It is best to rent various grinders to start with and see how you do.

Pay great attention to the serious business of safety. You need goggles to guard your eyes against fragments of stone, metal, and dust; a dust mask to protect your lungs from stone dust; ear protectors to shield your ears from noise; gloves to ward off splinters; and sturdy boots to armor your feet.

When you are ready to make a cut, switch on the power and move the machine forward, all the time remaining ready to resist kickback.

Choosing and fitting the cutting disc

Select a stone-cutting disc to fit your grinder. Disconnect the power cable, turn the spindle over by hand, and press in the lock button until the spindle stays put. Unscrew the clamping ring, slide on the correct disc, replace the ring, and use the special wrench to tighten up. Release the lock button and turn over the disc by hand to ensure it does not wobble or scrape. When you are happy that everything is correctly and safely assembled, you are ready to turn on the power and make the cut.

The correct working set-up

When using an angle grinder, it is a good idea to ask a helper to be present in case of any problems. First, establish a working area on the lawn and ban children and pets.

Set the slab to be worked on the ground. Make sure that none of your helpers is standing in front of the line of cut. Keep your feet well away from the cutting line. On no account kneel in line with the cutter, in case it slips. Never try to force the pace of the machine, and never twist the disc. If the cutting wheel looks in any way chipped, cracked, or warped, change to a new disc.

Guard
Never remove the guard

Leather gloves
Wear gloves to protect your hands from grit

Side handle
Maintain a firm grip on both the side handle and main handle

Cutting disc
Use a stone-cutting disc and ensure that it is in good condition

ABOVE Take the utmost care when using an angle grinder: it is a potentially dangerous tool. Follow safety procedures carefully.

Cutting procedure

1 Set the slab down flat on the grass and draw out the line of cut with a tape measure, chalk, and straight-edge. Check that the grinder is in good working order, and put on goggles, a dust mask, thick leather gloves, and sturdy boots. It is advisable to wear ear protectors too.

2 Hold the grinder so that the wheel is at a right angle to the slab. Brace yourself and, keeping your feet well out of the way, switch on the power. Hold the spinning disc to the chalk line and carefully make a light, scoring cut.

3 Make several runs to deepen the line of cut, then switch off the power and flip the slab over on the grass. Switch the power back on and rerun the whole procedure on the other side. Continue repeating the process until the slab breaks into two.

CUTTING STONE USING CHISELS

Using the bolster chisel

Bolster chisels are used for breaking and cutting stone. Purchase the best chisel that you can find – ideally one that has been drop-forged, hardened and tempered, and fitted with a one-piece molded plastic protective grip. Take the drill hammer and a piece of stone and experiment with various cuts and blows. The first thing you will observe is that the angle of the chisel, in relation to the weight of the blow, is critical to the cut. For example, a light, tentative tap with the chisel held at a right angle to the stone will result in a chip, while a heavy, decisive blow will result in a fracture. If you want to trim an edge, you angle the chisel toward the edge, lower it slightly, then make the blow. The edge will break away, leaving a peak on the edge face. By adjusting the angle of the chisel, it is possible to change the shape of the edge peak.

Using the cold chisel

Cold chisels are used for more delicate cutting tasks than bolster chisels. Purchase a top-quality 1-inch-wide (25 mm) chisel – choose one that has been drop-forged, hardened, and tempered. Support a slab of stone on a pad and use the drill hammer to try out various cuts. To trim an edge, hold the chisel at a very low angle to the stone, with the cutting edge looking to the edge of the stone, then make a light blow so that the waste breaks away as a chip rather than a chunk. Experiment with various angles and the weight of strike until you can, to some extent, predict the outcome.

Sharpening chisels

Drag and roll the end of the chisel against the grindstone until the ragged edge has been ground to a mitered bevel. Grind the cutting edge back to the original angle of about 60 degrees, continually dipping the tool into water to prevent the steel from overheating.

Cutting a stone in two

1 Chalk the line of cut on both sides of the stone and put the stone on something soft to help absorb the shock – such as a pad of old carpet, a pile of sand, or the lawn. Make sure that you are wearing goggles and strong leather gloves.

2 Take a bolster chisel in one hand and a drill hammer in the other and make a series of light passes to score the line. Do this three times, all the while increasing the power of the blows.

3 Repeat the procedure on the other side of the stone, then after about three passes, strike the chisel with maximum force until the stone breaks along the line.

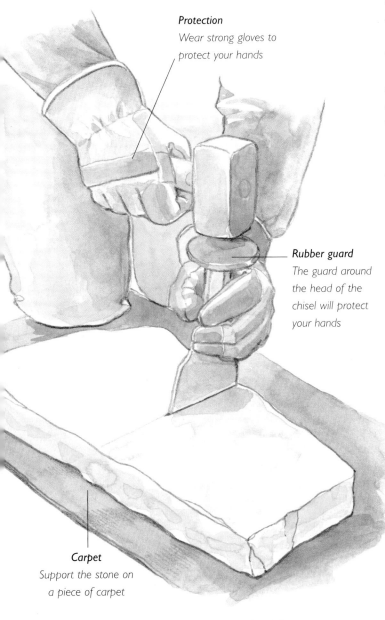

Protection
Wear strong gloves to protect your hands

Rubber guard
The guard around the head of the chisel will protect your hands

Carpet
Support the stone on a piece of carpet

ABOVE **Cutting stone using a bolster chisel and drill hammer.** Hold the chisel firmly on the mark and deliver a well-aimed blow.

HOW TO AVOID TOO MUCH CUTTING

Fitting is better than cutting

The secret of good stonework is, as far as possible, to use the stone as you find it. Choose your stone with great care, spending a long time selecting pieces for the best possible fit. If you work in this way, all you will have to do is to slightly modify edges and corners so that the pieces fit snugly alongside one another. Always try to fit rather than cut.

Striking blows

When you have decided on the position of the cutting line, set the edge of the chisel on the mark and strike it with a drill hammer. Repeat this procedure until the cut has been made. A single, well-aimed blow with the hammer is many times more effective than lots of little misaligned taps.

Working with the grain

Study the stone carefully and identify the grain, or strata lines. Try, as far as possible, to align your cuts with the run of the grain. This ensures the stone cuts cleanly.

Making foundations

Every stone structure starts with a foundation, ranging from gravel to crushed stone, compacted hardcore, and concrete. This section shows you how to select the option that suits your needs. It is important not to skimp on quantities. If in doubt, make a foundation bigger rather than smaller.

TYPES OF GROUND AND FOUNDATION REQUIREMENTS

Inspecting the site

Have a good look at the site. Dig a small hole to see what it is like under the topsoil. Is it hard and rocky, or is it soft and squashy? Is there a lot of rock and rubble on site? Is it well drained or boggy? In light of your survey, and in the knowledge that the options for a foundation range from a trench filled with gravel, to a trench with compacted hardcore and a layer of stone, or a trench with compacted hardcore and a layer of concrete, or various combinations of these, spend time considering your needs.

For example, if you wanted to build the Camomile Bench on page 114, and you have a dry, rocky site, you could get away with a 3-inch (80 mm) slab of concrete and a shallow layer of concrete. But on a wet site, you would need to dig a trench about 1 foot (300 mm) deep, half-fill it with gravel for drainage, then top it off with a generous layer of concrete.

If you are unsure what sort of drainage your site has, dig a trial hole, fill it with water, and see how long it takes to drain away.

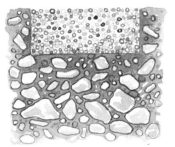

LEFT A gravel footpath needs no foundation if it is set in a well-drained, compacted soil. The gravel is adequately contained.

LEFT A compacted hardcore foundation for a concrete footpath. This is suitable for soil with moderate drainage.

CONSTRUCTING A CONCRETE SLAB FOUNDATION

Building procedure

1 Carefully measure the site, bang in wooden pegs to mark the limits of the foundation, and run a string around the pegs. Remove the sod and dig down to a depth of about 10 inches (250 mm). Clean the trench out to a level base. Move all the sod and the loose soil from the site.
2 Bang two wooden pegs into the trench base, positioned away from the sides as shown, so that they stand proud by about 8 inches (200 mm). They are about 2 inches (50 mm) below the sod level. Bridge the pegs with a level and adjust until they are at the same level. Try not to destroy the top of the pegs when hammering.
3 Half-fill the trench with hardcore and, being careful not to knock the pegs, compact it with a sledgehammer. Finally, top off the trench with concrete and tamp it level with a wooden beam. You should just be able to see the top of the pegs.

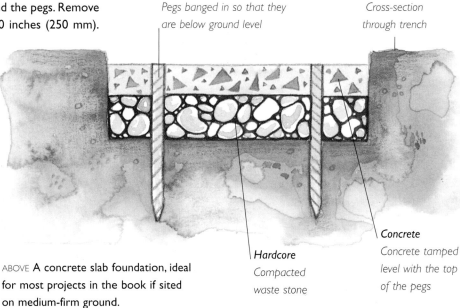

Peg
Pegs banged in so that they are below ground level

Soil
Cross-section through trench

ABOVE A concrete slab foundation, ideal for most projects in the book if sited on medium-firm ground.

Hardcore
Compacted waste stone

Concrete
Concrete tamped level with the top of the pegs

A ROCK AND RUBBLE FOUNDATION

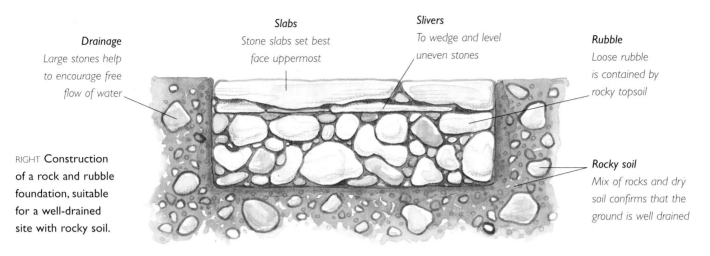

Drainage
Large stones help
to encourage free
flow of water

Slabs
Stone slabs set best
face uppermost

Slivers
To wedge and level
uneven stones

Rubble
Loose rubble
is contained by
rocky topsoil

RIGHT **Construction**
of a rock and rubble
foundation, suitable
for a well-drained
site with rocky soil.

Rocky soil
Mix of rocks and dry
soil confirms that the
ground is well drained

If you have a well-drained, rocky site with a thin layer of topsoil and a lot of loose stone and builder's rubble available, and you intend to build a project such as the the Dry-Stone Retaining Wall (page 88), you can easily get away without laying a concrete slab. Dig a trench to a depth of about 1 foot (300 mm), then systematically fill it with rock and rubble, all the while pounding it with the sledgehammer. When you get to within about 4 inches (100 mm) of ground level, carefully select large slabs of stone to cover the hardcore. Use small slivers and wedges of stone to adjust the level of the slabs so that they are firm and stable.

OTHER FOUNDATION EXAMPLES

If you have a well-drained site, you can lay a minimal foundation and top it off with a concrete slab. Let's say that you want to build the Pedestal Table on page 120. Dig a hole to a depth of about 16 inches (400 mm) and knock in four side pegs. Nail wooden battens to bridge pairs of pegs, keeping them at the same level, and finish up with the battens just below sod level. Half-fill the trench with hardcore, then fill with concrete up to the level of the battens. Drag a tamping beam across to skim the concrete level. Be careful not to knock the pegs or the battens out of alignment.

If you have a boggy site, you need to keep the foundation drained by digging two trenches for the hardcore. These are bridged and topped with a concrete slab.

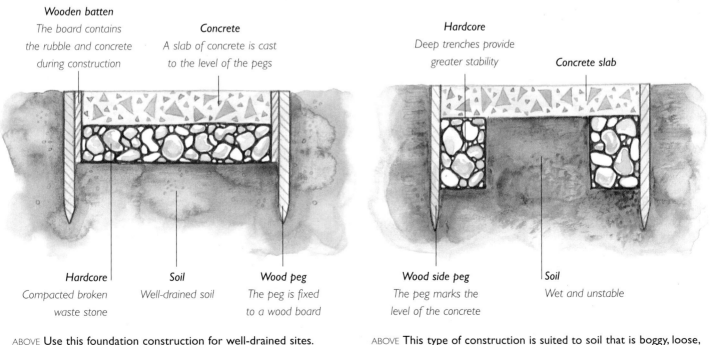

Wooden batten
The board contains
the rubble and concrete
during construction

Concrete
A slab of concrete is cast
to the level of the pegs

Hardcore
Deep trenches provide
greater stability

Concrete slab

Hardcore
Compacted broken
waste stone

Soil
Well-drained soil

Wood peg
The peg is fixed
to a wood board

Wood side peg
The peg marks the
level of the concrete

Soil
Wet and unstable

ABOVE **Use this foundation construction for well-drained sites. The surrounding soil needs to be reasonably compact and stable.**

ABOVE **This type of construction is suited to soil that is boggy, loose, and generally unstable. The hardcore walls provide good drainage.**

Paving and paths

Paving and paths not only enhance the garden in the sense that they are functionally desirable, they can also be visually exciting in terms of materials. Paths lead the eye – a path winding out of sight behind a hedge invites exploration and can impart an air of mystery. If you want to know more, keep reading.

DESIGNS FOR PATHS

ABOVE A gravel path edged with concrete "stone" blocks, which are supported by banked earth borders. The length of the curb blocks defines the shape of the curve.

ABOVE Reconstituted stones or flagstones framed by rows of bricks set on their edge. There is plenty of design scope with various combinations of materials and patterns.

ABOVE Randomly shaped stepping-stones make an attractive feature and are less intrusive than a solid path. The spaces between them must be equal.

Functional paths and paving

Have a look at your garden and consider how it might benefit from having one or more functional paths, or perhaps an area of utility paving. Perhaps you have trouble pushing your wheelbarrow down an existing path because it is too narrow? Would the vegetable garden be easier to work if it were divided up by a number of paths? Would it be a good idea to create a path along the shortest route from the back door to the compost heap? Do you want to avoid having to tiptoe across a muddy lawn? Do you wish that a particular area was dry so that children could play on it? Do you want a path wide enough for a wheelchair?

Designer paths and paving

The purpose of a designer path is not necessarily to take the shortest possible route, or even to provide a surface that is smooth and dry, but rather to provide the user with an exciting,

dynamic, tactile, and visual experience. Ideas such as irregular stepping-stones that curve across the lawn and disappear behind a shrub, the feel and sound of gravel underfoot, an area of paving that is decorated with an inset design, a paved circle with a bench seat – all encourage visitors to change pace and appreciate their surroundings. Well thought-out designer paths and areas of paving can enhance the landscape, adding shape, color, texture, and mystery to the composition of the garden.

Think how a path or an area of paving might improve your enjoyment of the garden. A paved circle would allow you to sit outside on a warm summer's evening. Or you could build a crazy paving path to wander around the rock garden and on to a camomile bench. Maybe you could design a combined path and paved circle, which could include a stone seat and barbecue. Your challenge may be a path that encircles the house, or a path that wanders off into the woods. The possibilities are endless.

FLAGSTONE PATH CONSTRUCTION

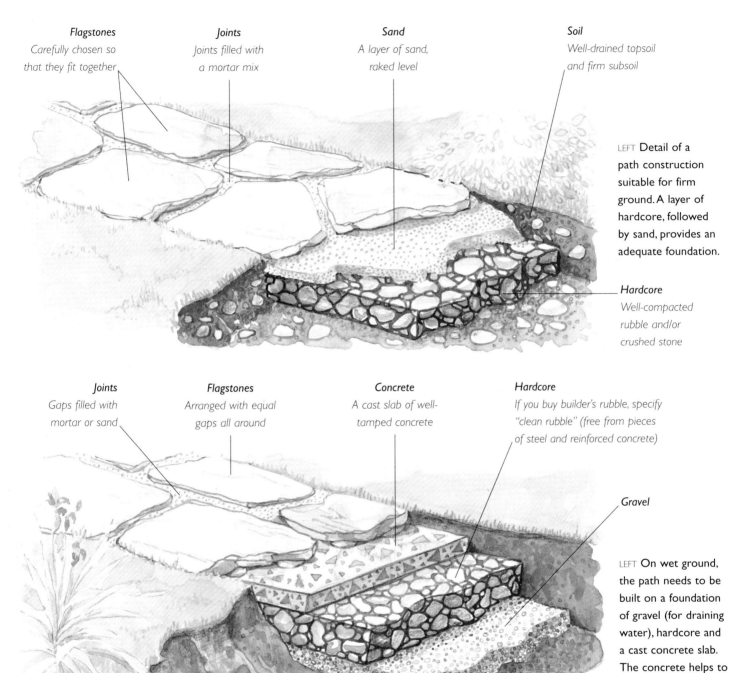

Flagstones
Carefully chosen so
that they fit together

Joints
Joints filled with
a mortar mix

Sand
A layer of sand,
raked level

Soil
Well-drained topsoil
and firm subsoil

LEFT Detail of a
path construction
suitable for firm
ground. A layer of
hardcore, followed
by sand, provides an
adequate foundation.

Hardcore
Well-compacted
rubble and/or
crushed stone

Joints
Gaps filled with
mortar or sand

Flagstones
Arranged with equal
gaps all around

Concrete
A cast slab of well-
tamped concrete

Hardcore
If you buy builder's rubble, specify
"clean rubble" (free from pieces
of steel and reinforced concrete)

Gravel

LEFT On wet ground,
the path needs to be
built on a foundation
of gravel (for draining
water), hardcore and
a cast concrete slab.
The concrete helps to
spread the load.

Flagstone paths on firm ground

If the ground is stony and well drained and you plan to use good-size flagstones, it is only necessary to build a foundation of waste stone topped off with a layer of sand.

Dig a trench to a depth of 8 inches (200 mm) and half-fill it with well-compacted builder's rubble or crushed stone to a thickness of 4 inches (100 mm). Top this with a 2-inch-thick (50 mm) bed of well-raked, level sand, then set the stones in place. Brush sand, with a mixture of grass and flower seeds, between the joints. The ingress of plants will help bind the stones firmly together.

Flagstone paths on wet ground

When the ground is soft and badly drained, and you want to use flagstones, you need to build a foundation of gravel covered by well-compacted hardcore and concrete.

Dig a trench to a depth of 10 inches (250 mm) and fill it with gravel to a thickness of 2 inches (50 mm). Spread builder's rubble or crushed stone on top to a thickness of 4 inches (100 mm). Top the hardcore with a 2-inch-thick (50 mm) bed of well-tamped concrete and set the stone in place. Brush sand between the joints. The gravel base will allow water to drain under the path.

Rock gardens

The whole subject of building rock gardens and arranging stone is so subjective that it is difficult to offer advice.

Go and look at other gardens, touch as many stones as you can, take a trip to a rocky beach or a mountain slope

to get inspiration from the natural landscape, and then decide what appeals to you.

ROCK GARDEN DESIGN AND SITING

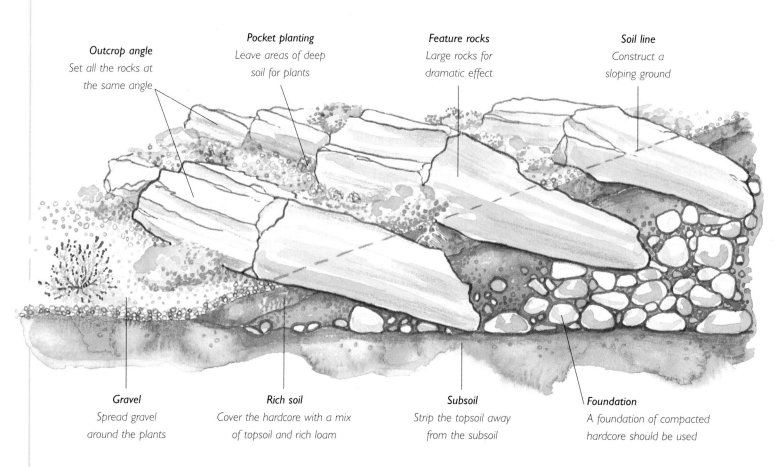

Outcrop angle
Set all the rocks at
the same angle

Pocket planting
Leave areas of deep
soil for plants

Feature rocks
Large rocks for
dramatic effect

Soil line
Construct a
sloping ground

Gravel
Spread gravel
around the plants

Rich soil
Cover the hardcore with a mix
of topsoil and rich loam

Subsoil
Strip the topsoil away
from the subsoil

Foundation
A foundation of compacted
hardcore should be used

Rock garden design

A good rock garden looks as if it is just the tip of a massive outcrop of stone that is hidden away under the ground. Do not attempt to build a rock garden from hand-size stones, arranging them haphazardly in an unlikely position, such as close to a lush border or around a swimming pool. It is much better to use a small number of large, well-weathered feature rocks and to site them so that they rear up through an otherwise controlled area, such as a gravel bed or lawn.

Stone groups

Groups of rocks or large stones are sometimes likened to families, and through the centuries, they have often inspired folk tales. When these large rocks are set together in an otherwise rock-free landscape, they seem to invite questions and attention and

cannot easily be ignored. Try this out for yourself on a slightly smaller scale by grouping three big stones together on your lawn. Family, friends, and neighbors will be sure to comment.

Standing guardians

Many societies have a tradition of erecting lone standing stones, for example the Japanese, the Chinese, and the Celts of ancient Britain. In the form of a monolithic slab set in the ground, such stones are almost invariably thought of as being guardians or sentinels. They are used to represent power, strength, permanence, and dignity. If you want something similar in your own garden, the only problem with stones of this size is how to move them into position. If you do not have access to a tractor and hoist, ask a dozen or so friends to help and move the stones with ropes, planks and rollers, a metal tube A-frame, and a car winch.

OTHER TYPES OF ROCK GARDEN

Gravel and stone garden

A gravel and stone garden can be formal, with low walls, a tight pattern of stones, and a bed of gravel to cover the ground. Alternatively, it can be informal, with a natural spread of stones and graded gravel to suggest a riverbed or scree. Start by planning out the paths, then cover the site with woven plastic sheet (to prevent weeds growing but allow drainage). Arrange a few good-size stones, then spread rivers of graded gravel and grit.

Grass and stone garden

To create a grass and stone garden, set three or four large stones (like islands) in a cropped lawn. Try various groupings for the stones and then, when you are happy with the layout, experiment by leaving selected areas of grass uncut. If there are wild meadow flowers growing in the long grass, and perhaps a sheltered space to sit in, or a flat slab of stone for a table, so much the better.

Pit and stone garden

One of the joys of walking in the country is coming across a secret, quiet place that nobody else seems to know about. We once found a little dell, with a circle of rocks, several grassy mounds, and a sunken area in between. The dell appeared to be the site of something that had fallen into decay. Perhaps it was once an old house, an ancient village, or a well.

You can achieve a similar effect by digging a shallow hole in the lawn, grassing over the resulting mounds of soil, and grouping a few feature stones around the site.

ABOVE A gravel and stone garden. Spread the gravel so that it flows around the larger stones like a riverbed.

ABOVE Grass and stone garden. Let the grass around the stones grow long and mow a passageway between the mounds.

PLANTING A ROCK GARDEN

Rock plants need a soil made of one part fine gravel or grit, one part sand, and one part garden loam. Assess your soil to see whether it is alkaline or acidic and purchase plants accordingly. For lime-loving rock plants, use this basic soil mix and scatter handfuls of flaked limestone around the site. Acid-loving plants will appreciate the addition of finely chopped bark instead.

Deep earth pocket

Small earth pocket
This will dry out easily, so use only for planting drought-resistant plants

LEFT Choose plants that thrive in dry, well-drained conditions. Depending on your soil type, plant lime- or acid-loving plants.

Deep earth pocket
There is plenty of room for a plant's root system, so it will sustain fairly large plants

Walls and other structures

An old proverb says, "A wall without a gate is a prison, while a wall with a gate is a paradise." Building a stone wall is a wonderfully creative and fulfilling experience: One moment you have a space and the next you have a structure! It may be a practical wall to keep the children in or a grand wall to make a statement.

DIFFERENT TYPES OF WALL

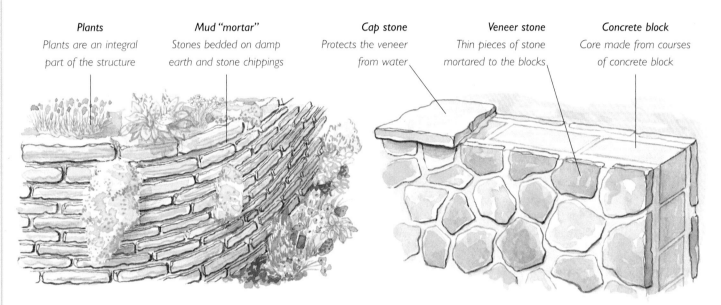

Plants
Plants are an integral part of the structure

Mud "mortar"
Stones bedded on damp earth and stone chippings

Cap stone
Protects the veneer from water

Veneer stone
Thin pieces of stone mortared to the blocks

Concrete block
Core made from courses of concrete block

ABOVE Dry-stone retaining wall. The horizontal courses must be kept in line and the vertical joints staggered. The plants help bond the wall together because the roots run back into the retained soil.

ABOVE Veneered wall. Stones are arranged in a pattern that fits together well and bedded in mortar. The stones are fixed one line at a time, leaving the mortar to stiffen before the next line is started.

Dry-stone walls

Dry-stone walls are traditionally made from whatever stone happens to be around, such as fieldstone, stone from the local quarry, or stone from a riverbed. Dry-stone walls always look at home in their surroundings for the simple reason that their color and texture blend with the landscape in which they are found. In cross-section, dry-stone walls always taper in from a wide base, with low walls sitting directly on the ground, and high walls starting in a trench well below frost level. The walls may be topped off with coping stones on edge, stones laid flat, a layer of concrete and cobbles, or even a mix of stones, loose earth, and sod.

Retaining walls

A retaining wall is best defined as a low wall that is used to hold back earth. Such walls are usually built on a sloping site where there is a need to step the ground to make a terrace. If you want to terrace a steep slope, it is better to go for a series of low walls rather than one or two high ones. Where the earth is heavy and wet, the foundation is created in a deep trench, the wall is made extra wide at the foot, and as much rock spoil as possible is heaped behind the wall to supply extra drainage.

Mortared walls

Mortared walls are usually built on a concrete foundation. The courses are made from "ashlar" (cut and shaped stone) or rubble (uncut fieldstone). However, many mortared walls are made from salvaged cut stone and carefully selected fieldstone. There are four rules for building this type of wall: Always rake back the mortar to reveal as much of the stone as possible, use a mortar that contains a good proportion of lime, make sure the mortar is stiff, and always wet the stone just before bonding. If you have any concerns about your wall-building project, such as getting the proportions of the mortar mix right, finding the color or absorption rate of your chosen stone, deciding on the depth of the courses, or the precise siting of the wall in the garden, it is a good idea to start off by building a small trial section of wall.

CAUTION

Make sure that all stone structures are strong, stable, and adequately reinforced. Until you are experienced, don't attempt to build structures that are taller than you.

HOW TO BUILD A STRAIGHT WALL

Building procedure

1 Dig a trench to a depth of between 10–12 inches (200–300 mm) and lay a foundation of compacted rubble topped with concrete (see page 24). Use a level at all stages to ensure that everything is level.

2 Lay a course of stones, selecting and cutting stones to achieve best fit, for the whole length of the wall. Do your best to make sure that the stones are all of more or less equal thickness.

3 Put the stones carefully to one side, wet them, and spread a generous layer of mortar over the foundation slab. Bed the stones in place on the mortar and tap them down with the hammer. Make sure that the second course is well staggered against the first.

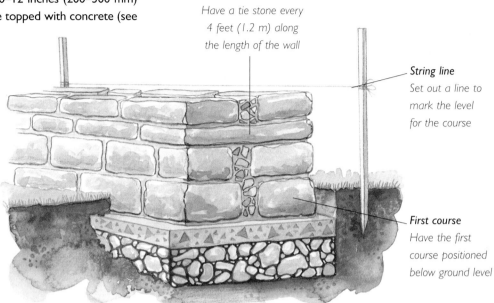

Tie stones
Have a tie stone every 4 feet (1.2 m) along the length of the wall

String line
Set out a line to mark the level for the course

First course
Have the first course positioned below ground level

PILLARS AND PIERS

Building a pillar

The techniques for building piers, square-section pillars, and round-section pillars are similar. Building a round-section pillar, however, is a wonderful, skill-stretching experience that should not be missed. You are forever doing your best to fit the individual stones so that they run as close as possible to the circular section plan. It is best to practice laying a course of stones without

mortar first of all (all the stones that fit the edge of the circle, and then all the stones to fill in). Next, put them to one side, spread the mortar, and bed the selected and trimmed stones in place. Tap down the whole layer of stones with a trowel or hammer, check the horizontal and vertical truth with a level, make adjustments, then move on to the next course. If the courses bulge, stop building until the mortar has cured.

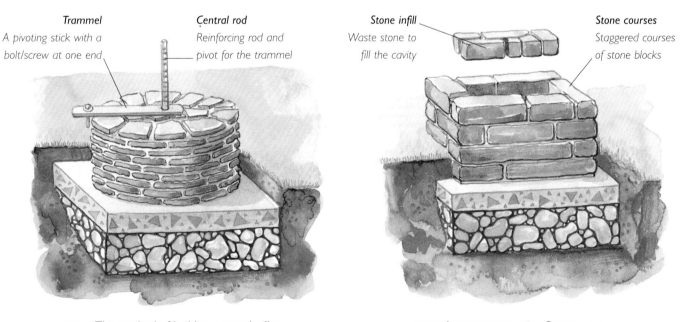

Trammel
A pivoting stick with a bolt/screw at one end

Central rod
Reinforcing rod and pivot for the trammel

Stone infill
Waste stone to fill the cavity

Stone courses
Staggered courses of stone blocks

ABOVE This method of building a round pillar uses a central rod and a trammel (a stick that is rotated to check the circumference).

ABOVE A square stone pier. Courses are established and then infilled with waste stone. All the vertical joints are staggered.

Part 2: **Projects**

Stepping-stone path

Rough-cut stepping-stones make a delightful path that is perfect for light foot traffic, great for children playing jumping games, and also suitable for pushing a wheelbarrow on. The flow of stones meandering across the lawn fulfills a design function, too, beautifully leading the eye from one garden feature to another.

<table>
<tr><td>

TIME

About half a day (for nine medium-size stones).

</td></tr>
<tr><td>

SAFETY

Setting the stones is a difficult, finger-nipping task, so make sure that you wear thick leather gloves.

</td></tr>
</table>

YOU WILL NEED

Materials *for a path with nine stepping-stones*
- Flagstones: 9 salvaged slate or limestone flags about 20 in (500 mm) long, 16 in (400 mm) wide, and 2 in (50 mm) thick
- Soft sand: about 1 bucket of sand per stone

Tools
- Wheelbarrow
- Spade
- Fork
- Bucket
- Wooden tamping beam: about 20 in (500 mm) long, 2½ in (60 mm) wide, and 2 in (50 mm) thick
- Sledgehammer

SITING THE PATH

Before you decide where to put the path, think about the ebb and flow of traffic in the garden. Work out how many times during your day-to-day activities you walk from one point to another. For example, when you empty the kitchen waste onto the compost heap, do you always take the same route? Do you avoid certain routes because the ground is muddy? Are there any worn areas on the lawn, which indicate heavy wear? They will be dusty and bald in summer, muddy and dipped in winter.

When you have considered all the options and variables, map out the best route for the path. Before you calculate the number of stones and their spacing, take into account the length of stride of the people most likely to use the path. Have a trial "stepping out" across the lawn to work out the required spacing. When you come to choosing the stones, it does not matter if they are different sizes and odd shapes, or even if there are great variations in thickness, as long as each stone has one sound, level face.

PLAN VIEW OF PATH

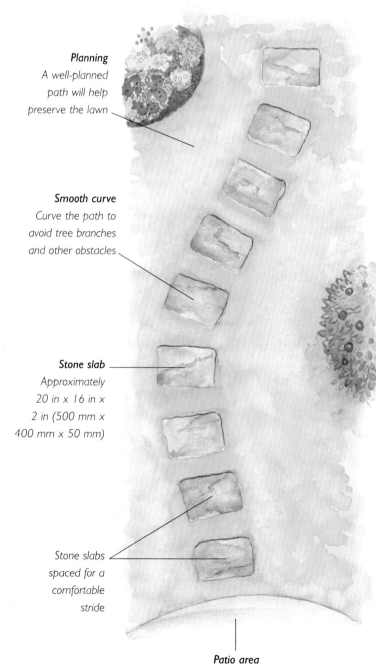

Planning
A well-planned path will help preserve the lawn

Smooth curve
Curve the path to avoid tree branches and other obstacles

Stone slab
Approximately 20 in x 16 in x 2 in (500 mm x 400 mm x 50 mm)

Stone slabs spaced for a comfortable stride

Patio area

CROSS-SECTION THROUGH PATH

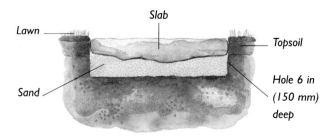

Slab

Lawn

Topsoil

Sand

Hole 6 in (150 mm) deep

Step-by-step: **Making the stepping-stone path**

Spacing
Check that the spacing
suits your length of stride

Best face
Make sure that
the best face of
the flagstone is
uppermost

I Set out the flagstones on the lawn, spacing them to suit the stride of the people who will use the path. Experiment with various alignments – curved, straight, or winding – until you are pleased with the overall effect. Arrange the individual flags so that the best face is uppermost.

Helpful hint

If, when you're putting the stones down, you notice that any layers are starting to separate slightly with handling, it is a sign that the stone is not very stable and would wear rapidly. Reject it and replace with another.

Alignment
Adjust the flagstones so that
they are aligned with each other

Lifting sod
A round-pronged fork
is good for this

Depth
Aim for a
recess about
6 in (150 mm)
deep

Sod
Only pick up as
much sod as
you can lift
comfortably

2 Use a small, clean, sharp spade to cut into the ground around each stone. Hold the spade upright and cut to a depth of about 8 inches (200 mm), making sure that the cuts cross over at the corners. Repeat this for all the stones in the line.

3 Carefully lift the stone to one side. Quarter the defined sod with the spade, use the fork to lift the quarters into the wheelbarrow, and take to the compost heap. With the spade, excavate the recess to an overall depth of 6 inches (150 mm).

Hole depth
Make adjustments to holes to
suit varying thicknesses of stone

Stone height
The stone needs to be ½ in
(10 mm) lower than the lawn

Corners
Clean the
earth from
the corners of
the holes

Lawn
Try not to
damage the
edge of
the lawn

Sand
Spread sand
over the recess

4 Work along the line of flagstones, removing the sod and soil, until you have a line of holes that fit the stones. Pay particular attention to the corners of the holes – they need to be crisp and clean.

5 Gauge the thickness of the stone and the depth of the hole, spread sand to a depth of 3–3½ inches (80–90 mm), then bed the stone in place. (Lift the stone and adjust the sand until the flagstone is about ½ inch [10 mm] lower than the lawn.)

Sledgehammer
Let the shaft of the hammer
slide through your hands

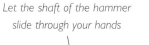

6 When the flagstone is nicely bedded on the sand, place the wooden beam diagonally across it and use the sledgehammer to gently tamp the stone into place. If the stone tilts or sinks, simply lift one edge and adjust the level of the sand.

Footwork
Hold the beam
secure with
your feet

Depth
If the slab does
not sit level,
remove it and
adjust the sand
underneath

Cobble spiral

Cobbles set in concrete make a great decorative feature that can be employed to direct the movement of cars on your driveway. The spaced cobbles are slightly uncomfortable to drive over, so visitors will instinctively steer around them. If you would like to enhance your drive with a feature that is attractive, hard wearing, and functional, cobbles are wonderfully suitable.

TIME

A day to build, seven days for the concrete to cure.

SAFETY

Don't strain your back trying to lift a whole bag of cobbles. It is much better to open the bag and take out a few at a time.

YOU WILL NEED

Materials *for a circle 6 ft (1.8 m) in diameter*
- Hardcore: 3 wheelbarrow loads broken rubble or stone
- Concrete: 1 part (94 lb or 50 kg) cement, 2 parts (200 lb or 100 kg) sharp sand, 3 parts (350 lb or 150 kg) aggregate
- Cobbles: 100 lb of 3 in (50 kg of 80 mm) cobbles (allows for choice)
- Gravel: 50 lb of 1 in (25 kg of 25 mm) gravel (allows for choice)

Tools
- Tape measure and chalk
- Wheelbarrow
- Sledgehammer
- Mason's hammer
- Spade and shovel
- Bucket
- Wooden tamping beam: about 3 ft (900 mm) long, 4 in (100 mm) wide, and ¾ in (20 mm) thick
- Bricklayer's trowel

MARKING AND PLANNING

Decide on the size of the circle according to your driveway. Our circle has been made in an old flowerbed with an existing brick edging, but you could make a larger circle with a cobble edging (the radius of the circle should be no larger than you can reach).

Wash the cobbles, grade them from large to small, and have a trial dry run. With tape measure and chalk, mark out a circle on the drive, pinpointing the center. Transporting the cobbles in the wheelbarrow, position the biggest and best cobble at the center. Add further stones to make a spiral, working clockwise and finishing up with the smallest cobbles. Once the cobbles are in place, use the shingle to run a secondary spiral within the first.

We have increased the overall dynamic effect of the spiral by tamping the concrete to make a pattern that radiates out from the center. Once the concrete has been mixed, you have to work quickly before it sets. Finally, don't forget to place a barrier around the finished circle so that you don't drive over it by mistake while it is drying.

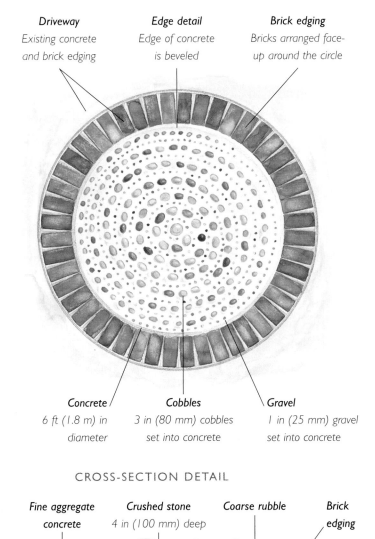

PLAN VIEW OF THE COBBLE SPIRAL

Driveway
Existing concrete and brick edging

Edge detail
Edge of concrete is beveled

Brick edging
Bricks arranged face-up around the circle

Concrete
6 ft (1.8 m) in diameter

Cobbles
3 in (80 mm) cobbles set into concrete

Gravel
1 in (25 mm) gravel set into concrete

CROSS-SECTION DETAIL

Coarse concrete *Fine aggregate concrete* *Crushed stone* 4 in (100 mm) deep *Coarse rubble* *Brick edging*

Step-by-step: **Making the cobble spiral**

Hardcore
Pound the hardcore in place
with the sledgehammer

Tamping
Work with a rapid
tapping action

Brick edge
Be careful not
to damage any
existing edging

Pivot
Pivot one
end of the
beam on the
center point

Radial pattern
Tamp the
concrete into a
radial pattern

1 Having marked out the circle, dig it out to a depth of about 7 inches (180 mm). (If you need to break up the concrete of the existing driveway, use the sledgehammer and mason's hammer to do so.) Shovel in the hardcore using the sledgehammer to pound it into place. The hardcore layer should be 4 inches (100 mm) deep.

2 Measure out the dry ingredients for the concrete (cement, sharp sand, and aggregate). Fill the bucket with water. Mix sufficient water into the dry ingredients to make the correct consistency of concrete. Shovel the concrete into place, then use the beam to bring it to the same level as the brick edging and tamp it into a radial pattern.

Trowel angle
Angle the trowel into
the brick edge

Cobbles
Grade the cobbles
into sizes

Smooth finish
Run the trowel
around until
the concrete is
smooth

Spiral
Arrange the
stones into
a smooth
spiral shape

Tapping
Allow the
weight of the
sledgehammer
to fall on
the cobble

3 Holding the bricklayer's trowel at a sharp angle and run it around the edge of the concrete. Do this a couple of times to achieve a smooth, beveled finish.

4 Select a good cobble for the center and use the weight of the sledgehammer to tap it very gently into place. Repeat the procedure with a dozen stones, establishing the pattern.

Damaged cobbles
Put damaged cobbles to
one side and avoid using

5 Continue setting out the cobbles, making sure they are aligned and then tamping them into place with the sledgehammer. Stand back periodically to check that the spiral relates evenly to the circle.

Trial placing
Set out about six cobbles at a time. Check for size and fit before you tap them into place

Spacing
Try to keep the spacing between the lines consistent

6 When you have placed all the cobbles, use the gravel to run a second spiral within the first. Use the mason's hammer to tap the pebbles into position. Leave the concrete to cure for seven days before driving on it.

Gravel
Run the line of gravel between the big cobbles

Helpful hint

Wash individual stones in water and set out a sequence of six or so stones at a time. Don't strike the stone, but rather let the weight of the hammer do most of the work. Continue gently tapping until the stone is slightly more than half buried in the concrete.

Natural outcrop rock garden

A swift and easy way to add a dynamic feature to an otherwise level expanse of lawn is to build a rock garden that looks like a natural outcrop. Rocks breaking through the ground suggest powerful, dynamic forces at work within the garden, while the well-drained environment allows you to cultivate a broad range of plants.

TIME

A weekend to build, two days of good weather for arranging the stones and for planting.

SAFETY

Moving large stones is hard, dangerous work – get someone to help you.

YOU WILL NEED

Materials *for a rock garden 10 ft x 8 ft x 2 ft (3 m x 2.4 m x 600 mm)*
- Soil: 1 ton (5 parts good-quality topsoil to 1 part sharp sand)
- Feature rocks: 6 large sandstone rocks (the biggest you are able to move)
- Split sandstone: approximately 1 ton (for foundation stones and decorative edging)

- Secondary rocks: 6 medium-size sandstone rocks
- Alpine grit: 50 lb (25 kg) crushed granite
- Oyster shell grit: 50 lb (25 kg) well-washed crushed shell

Tools
- Fork
- Wheelbarrow
- Spade
- Drill hammer
- Gardening trowel

A ROCK AND HEATHER MIX

Study the garden and think about the various options for the positioning of the rocks. Do you want to have an island surrounded by a sea of lawn, or are you going to build it as a peninsular feature that divides two areas of lawn? Are you going to buy the topsoil and build the rock garden as a self-contained feature, or are you going to use earth moved from another project? (If you can use earth left over from another project, such as a pond excavation, or the topsoil removed prior to building an extension to the house, you save both time and money.)

The task of moving the rocks and earth is a major part of this project. Ideally, you need to plan the whole operation so that they have to be shifted only a short distance. Use a wheelbarrow and ask a friend to help you maneuver heavy rocks (see page 21).

It is preferable to choose a site for the rock garden that is well away from formal borders so that it does not create an imbalance between the various plantings in the garden. When we designed this feature, we had in mind the sort of natural outcrop that you often see at the bottom of scree slopes, where rock and heather meet green pasture.

PLAN VIEW OF THE ROCK GARDEN

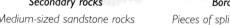

Grit
Alpine grit and oyster shell

Feature rocks
Large sandstone rocks

Wall

Split sandstone

Secondary rocks
Medium-sized sandstone rocks

Border
Pieces of split sandstone

CROSS-SECTION OF THE ROCK GARDEN

Soil
Pockets of soil between rocks

Feature rock

Secondary rock

Split sandstone

Step-by-step: Making the natural outcrop rock garden

Retaining wall
*Use an existing feature
as a retaining wall*

Pocket slope
*Angle the hole so that it
is deepest at the back*

Spreading soil
*Work the earth
with the fork
and your feet*

Pocket
*Dig a pocket
to match the
size of the
stone*

Trial fit
*You may need
several
attempts to get
the stone to fit
the hole*

1 With the fork, work the mound of earth to remove weeds, lumps of clay, and unwanted stones. Walk back and forth over the earth to collapse cavities and compact it into shape.

2 Load stones into the wheelbarrow and move them to the site. The large stones are grouped like a series of steps. Dig a pocket toward the bottom of the mound and carefully ease one of the largest feature stones into place.

Earth anchor
*Load earth on the tail
end of the stone*

Wedging
*Compact the
earth so the
front of the
stone rears up.
Wedge waste
stone under
the front of
the rock
to preserve
the angle*

3 When you are pleased with the overall position and angle of the feature stone, take some pieces of split sandstone and use the drill hammer to bang them under the stone. The sandstone will wedge the feature stone firmly in place.

Helpful hint

Compact the earth under the leading edge of the stone until the stone is rearing up at the front with the bulk of its weight at the tail end. Add fragments of waste stone (or old bricks, concrete, or hardcore) to the compacted earth.

Secondary stones
Use smaller stones to
complement the arrangement

Soil
Soil incorporates grit
for drainage

Outcrop angle
The stones
should rear
up at the
same angle

Stone angle
Trowel earth
under the
stone to adjust
the angle

Edging
Use stone on
edge to define
the garden

4 Work up the slope, repeating the procedure until you achieve a series of steps that slope back slightly into the mound. Trowel earth in and around the stones to hold them in place.

5 When you have completed the basic outcrop, with all the stones rearing up at the same angle, dig a trench around the mound and define it with an edging of split sandstone. Plant the garden.

Plant color
Choose plants that have
different seasons of interest

6 Finally, when you have completed your planting, scatter handfuls of alpine grit and crushed oyster shell in and around the plants and stones to cover the earth and help give the impression that the rock garden is part of a natural outcrop.

Watering
Water the
plants to settle
the roots

Alpine grit and oyster shell
The spread of grit and
oyster shell helps the earth
to retain moisture

Inspirations: Rock gardens

The contrast between large stones and minute plants is uniquely beautiful. However, rock gardens come in many shapes and sizes, from the austere sand and rock gardens of Japan to the little stone rock gardens that characterized English suburban landscapes in the 1920s and 1930s. Regardless of size, most rock gardens use stone and plants to suggest or replicate a natural setting. There are rock plants suitable for all situations, from exposed sites to crevices, and both sunny and shady positions.

RIGHT A flight of railroad tie steps has been transformed into an eye-catching feature simply by edging the steps with carefully chosen limestone rocks, spreading an infill of crushed stone between the wooden treads, and planting with species that thrive in a well-drained alkaline soil.

ABOVE A water rock garden of Welsh slate planted with dwarf conifers and alpines. This garden is reminiscent of high mountain passes, ice-cold springs, and tranquillity.

RIGHT A Feng Shui rock garden designed by Pamela Woods. Large feature rocks, gravel, wooden decking, and water create a sublimely peaceful garden space.

Tessellated paving

An exciting and creative way of repairing an existing paved patio is to replace damaged slabs with an infill pattern of tessellated tiles. All you do is remove the slabs, revealing the underlying base, then bed in the tiles with a skim of mortar.

TIME

A day and a half to build (eight hours for laying the tiles, and four hours for grouting and tidying up).

SAFETY

Cement (both dry and wet) can cause skin irritation and burns, so wear gloves for mixing.

YOU WILL NEED

Materials *for 2 areas of paving 3 ft (920 mm) square*
- Mortar: 2 parts (66 lb or 30 kg) cement, 1 part (33 lb or 15 kg) lime, 9 parts (300 lb or 135 kg) soft sand
- Concrete tiles (imitation terracotta): 8 lozenge tiles (20 in x 18 in or 510 mm x 215 mm), 22 small square tiles (6 in x 6 in or 150 mm x 150 mm), 1 large square tile (12 in x 12 in or 300 mm x 300 mm)
- Gravel: 50 lb (25 kg) washed gravel (½–1 in or 15–25 mm)

Tools
- Drill hammer
- Wheelbarrow
- Tape measure and chalk
- Bucket
- Spade and shovel
- Wooden tamping beam: about 16 in (400 mm) long, 2½ in (60 mm) wide, and 1 in (25 mm) thick
- Mortar float
- Bricklayer's trowel

PRETTY AS A PICTURE

In this project, the word "tessellate" refers to the act of grouping tiles so that they fit together like a mosaic or a tiled floor. Identical square tiles tessellate to make a checkerboard pattern, but more dynamic effects can be obtained when two or more different shapes are arranged to create an overall repeat pattern, like the lozenge-shaped and square tiles in our two designs.

We lifted eight concrete slabs to create two identical square recesses. To remove a slab, hit it in the middle with a drill hammer and pick the broken pieces out with a trowel. Note how we have used three shapes to fit the frame – a lozenge and two different squares – and then filled in around the tiles with a pattern of gravel. It is best to start with just a few shapes, playing around with various arrangements until you come up with an exciting design, and then to purchase additional tiles to suit your needs.

PLAN VIEW OF THE TESSELLATED PAVING

Gravel
Decorative gravel set in mortar

Small square tile
6 in x 6 in (150 x 150 mm)

Paved area
Existing paving slab surround

Large square tile
12 in x 12 in (300 x 300 mm)

Lozenge tile
20 in x 8½ in (510 x 215 mm)

CROSS-SECTION OF THE TESSELLATED PAVING

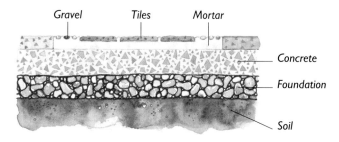

Gravel   Tiles   Mortar

Concrete

Foundation

Soil

Step-by-step: **Making the tessellated paving**

Existing slabs
Make sure existing slabs are stable

Corners
Make sure the mortar gets right into the corners

Tamping
Use a wooden beam to tamp the mortar level

Float
Work the float from side to side

Uniform bed
Aim for a smooth, level finish

1 Use the tape measure and chalk to draw guidelines on the concrete slabs. Sprinkle water over the exposed foundation, shovel the mortar into place, and tamp it level with the beam so that it ends up slightly lower than the slabs.

2 Use the mortar float to skim the mortar into the corners and right to the edges of the recess. Work the float from side to side to achieve a uniform bed with no cavities or bumps.

Center line
Make sure the tiles are aligned with the registration marks

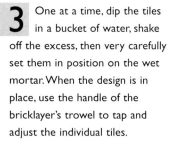

3 One at a time, dip the tiles in a bucket of water, shake off the excess, then very carefully set them in position on the wet mortar. When the design is in place, use the handle of the bricklayer's trowel to tap and adjust the individual tiles.

Tapping
Use the handle of the trowel to tap the tile in position

Wet the tiles
In hot weather sprinkle water over the tiles to hold back the drying time of the mortar

Tile level
Keep the tiles level with
the surrounding slabs

Bedding
Move the tile
from side to
side to bed it
in place

4 If, at any point along the way, a tile sinks too deeply or sticks up at an angle, lift it with the point of the trowel, add a little more mortar, then gently bed it back into place.

Helpful hint

If the day is sunny and the tiles feel hot and dry to the touch, soak the back of each tile in water just prior to bedding it into the mortar. Wiggle the tile rapidly on the spot until you feel it begin to settle.

Gravel patterns
Arrange the
gravel into a
pleasing pattern

5 Finally, when all the tiles are in position, use the gravel to make patterns in the remaining areas of mortar. Set the pebbles in one at a time. Leave for 24 hours before it is dry enough for light traffic, or seven days before it is ready for heavy use.

Cleaning
Use a damp
cloth to clean
the tiles and
remove spots
of mortar

Raised bed

A raised bed gives you the opportunity to add an extra planting area to your garden, and the change in level creates interest. You can build it on an existing patio or area of concrete. The good thing about raised beds is that you do not have to stoop to weed them. This one is built from double-sided reconstituted stone blocks.

TIME

A weekend to build (two full days to build on an existing patio base).

COMMENT

Reconstituted stone blocks are heavy and fragile. Handle the blocks with care, preferably wearing gloves.

YOU WILL NEED

Materials *for a bed 10 ft (1.10 m) square and 20 in (510 mm) high*
- Mortar: 2 parts (44 lb or 20 kg) cement, 1 part (22 lb or 10 kg) lime, 9 parts (200 lb or 90 kg) soft sand
- Double-sided "York stone" blocks: 48 blocks, 18 in (450 mm) long, 6 in (150 mm) wide, and 2½ in (65 mm) thick
- Straight "York stone"

coping blocks: 8 blocks, 18 in (450 mm) long, 7¼ in (185 mm) wide, and 2 in (47 mm) thick

Tools
- Wheelbarrow
- Tape measure and chalk
- Level and a length of batten
- Shovel
- Bucket
- Bricklayer's trowel
- Mason's hammer
- Pointing trowel
- Stiff brush

A BED ON THE PATIO

If you are looking for a project that involves a minimum of effort and expertise, this is a good one to try. The sizes specified for the wall blocks and coping blocks allow you to build a rectilinear form without the need for cutting. The clever design of the blocks means that all the exposed faces are textured.

This project is designed to be set directly onto a base of existing patio slabs, avoiding the need to build a foundation. The bed can be sited away from walls, so that it can be viewed and approached from all sides, or it can be against a wall. If you are going to put it near a building, make sure that there is enough space for you to move the blocks into position.

PLAN VIEW OF THE RAISED BED

CROSS-SECTION OF THE RAISED BED

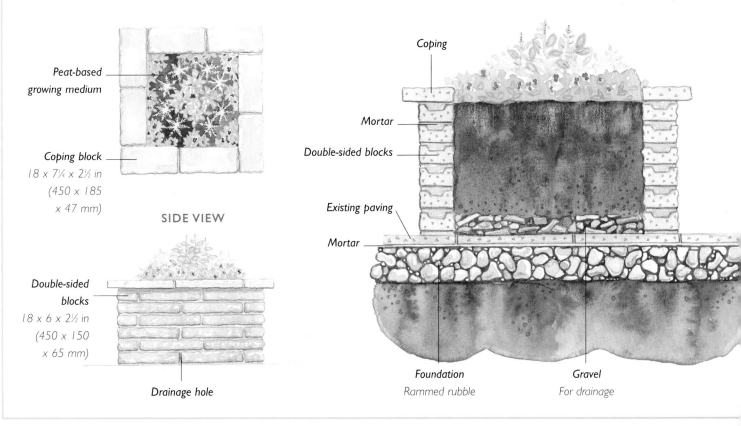

Peat-based growing medium

Coping block
18 x 7¼ x 2½ in (450 x 185 x 47 mm)

SIDE VIEW

Double-sided blocks
18 x 6 x 2½ in (450 x 150 x 65 mm)

Drainage hole

Coping

Mortar

Double-sided blocks

Existing paving

Mortar

Foundation
Rammed rubble

Gravel
For drainage

Step-by-step: Making the raised bed

Chalk lines
Use the chalk to set out guidelines

Level
Check with the level to see if the blocks are sitting level

Drainage
Leave one vertical course open on each side of the first course for a drainage hole

1 Use the tape measure, chalk, and level to establish the position of the bed. Use eight wall blocks to form the first course of the bed. Arrange them in position so that each side of the bed shows two long faces of the blocks and one end face.

Helpful hint

When you come to testing with the level, be aware that a vertical height difference of, say, ¼ in (5 mm) might be caused by no more than a blob of mortar. Wipe both the spirit level and the top of the blocks before taking a reading.

Buttering
Butter the end of the block with the mortar

Mortar bed
Lay down a generous bed of mortar

Mortar
Do not worry about mortar oozing out inside the bed

Tapping
Use the hammer to tap blocks into line

Staggered courses
Arrange the courses so that the blocks overlap joins

2 Use the bricklayer's trowel to lay down a bed of mortar. Dampen the blocks and patio slabs. Place a block on the mortar, butter the end of the next block with mortar and set it alongside. Continue in the same way for all eight blocks.

3 Check that the blocks are level with the level and the batten. Tap any blocks that stand proud with the mason's hammer. Repeat the procedure for the next course of blocks. Note how the pattern of blocks is staggered.

Sighting
Look down the wall and
tap blocks into position

Mortar
Clean the mortar off the top
before leveling

Checking
After each
course, check
that blocks
are level and
aligned

Leveling
Make sure that
both the batten
and the level
are free from
blobs of mortar

4 Continue laying one course of blocks upon another, all the while checking that they are horizontal with the level and batten, tapping blocks into place with the mason's hammer, and tidying up the mortar with the pointing trowel.

5 When you have built all six courses, rake out some of the mortar with the pointing trowel. Clean up with the stiff brush and check the overall squareness of the structure by setting the level across the corners. If you need to make adjustments, use the batten to tap blocks into place rather than the level.

Tapping
Use the trowel handle to tap
the blocks into final position

6 Finally, lay a bed of mortar on the top course and set the coping stones in place. Their back edge should be level with the inside face of the wall; the front edge forms a lip around the bed. Before filling the bed with soil, allow two days for the mortar to dry.

Bedding
Twist the block
slightly back
and forth while
applying light
pressure

Raking
Leave the raking
(scraping excess
mortar from
between the
blocks) until the
mortar is half-set

Flagstone steps

Flagstone steps are not only a practical and functional means of coping with a steep,

sloping garden, but are also a dynamic design feature in their own right. The steps

lead the eye from one level to another and suggest that there are other exciting

areas of garden still to be explored. This project consists of three steps.

TIME

A weekend to build three steps, seven days for the concrete and mortar to set before walking on the steps.

SPECIAL TIPS

The longer the concrete is kept moist during the curing (drying) process, the stronger it will be. Each day for seven days sprinkle the concrete with water. Keep the steps covered with a plastic sheet or old carpet.

CROSS-SECTION OF THE FLAGSTONE STEPS

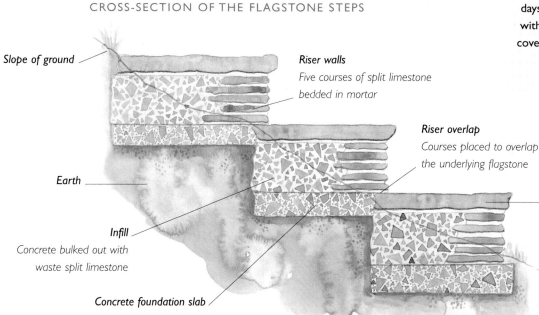

Slope of ground

Earth

Infill
Concrete bulked out with waste split limestone

Concrete foundation slab

Riser walls
Five courses of split limestone bedded in mortar

Riser overlap
Courses placed to overlap the underlying flagstone

Flagstone slab
Limestone or slate salvaged flagstone (best to have the worn side facing uppermost) bedded in mortar

YOU WILL NEED

Materials *For 3 steps, each 24 in (600 mm) wide, 16½ in (420 mm) deep, and 6¾ in (170 mm) high*
- Concrete: 1 part (94 lb or 40 kg) cement, 2 parts (175 lb or 80 kg) sharp sand, 3 parts (265 lb or 120 kg) aggregate
- Mortar: 2 parts (50 lb or 24 kg) cement, 1 part (25 lb or 12 kg) lime, 9 parts (240 lb or 108 kg) soft sand
- Slate or limestone flagstones: 3 salvaged flags, about 24 in (600 mm) long, 16½ in (420 mm) wide, and 1½ in (40 mm) thick

- Split limestone: 3 square yards (meters) salvaged roof stone, about ½ in (15 mm) thick

Tools
- Wheelbarrow and bucket
- Tape measure and chalk
- Spade and shovel
- Wooden beam for tamping: about 24 in (600 mm) long, 3 in (80 mm) wide, and 2 in (50 mm) thick
- Level
- Mason's hammer
- Bricklayer's trowel
- Drill hammer
- Pointing trowel

UP AND DOWN THE GARDEN

Study the site and visualize how the steps will relate to the overall layout of the garden – the slope of the land, other features within the garden, and underground structures, such as foundations and pipes. When the flagstones are in place, the treads measure no less than 16½ inches (420 mm) from the edge of the step to the riser. The riser walls are about 5 inches (125 mm) high, to give a total step height of no more than 6¾ inches (170 mm). Each step is constructed in four stages – laying the concrete foundation slab, building the riser wall, back-filling behind the riser wall, and setting the flagstone in place.

The concrete foundation slabs are made from a 1-2-3 mix – 1 part cement, 2 parts sharp sand, and 3 parts aggregate, and the infill is bulked out with waste stone. The mortar is a 2-1-9 mix – 2 parts cement, 1 part lime, and 9 parts soft sand. The riser walls are built from five courses of salvaged roof stone, with the best edges of the stone placed outward. Finally, while we have covered the cut-in ground at the sides of the steps with pieces of flint, you might prefer to use something different, such as gravel, found field-stone, sod, ground-cover plants, or crushed bark.

Flagstone steps

FRONT VIEW OF THE FLAGSTONE STEPS, INCLUDING CROSS-SECTION DETAIL

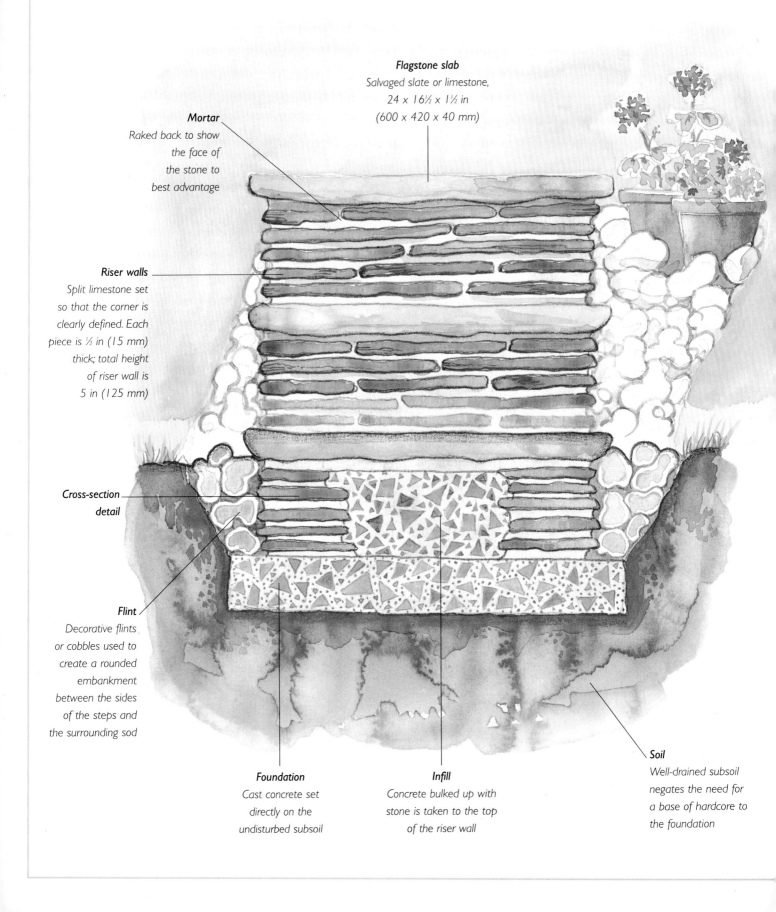

Mortar
Raked back to show
the face of
the stone to
best advantage

Flagstone slab
Salvaged slate or limestone,
24 x 16½ x 1½ in
(600 x 420 x 40 mm)

Riser walls
Split limestone set
so that the corner is
clearly defined. Each
piece is ½ in (15 mm)
thick; total height
of riser wall is
5 in (125 mm)

**Cross-section
detail**

Flint
Decorative flints
or cobbles used to
create a rounded
embankment
between the sides
of the steps and
the surrounding sod

Foundation
Cast concrete set
directly on the
undisturbed subsoil

Infill
Concrete bulked up with
stone is taken to the top
of the riser wall

Soil
Well-drained subsoil
negates the need for
a base of hardcore to
the foundation

PLAN VIEW OF THE FLAGSTONE STEPS

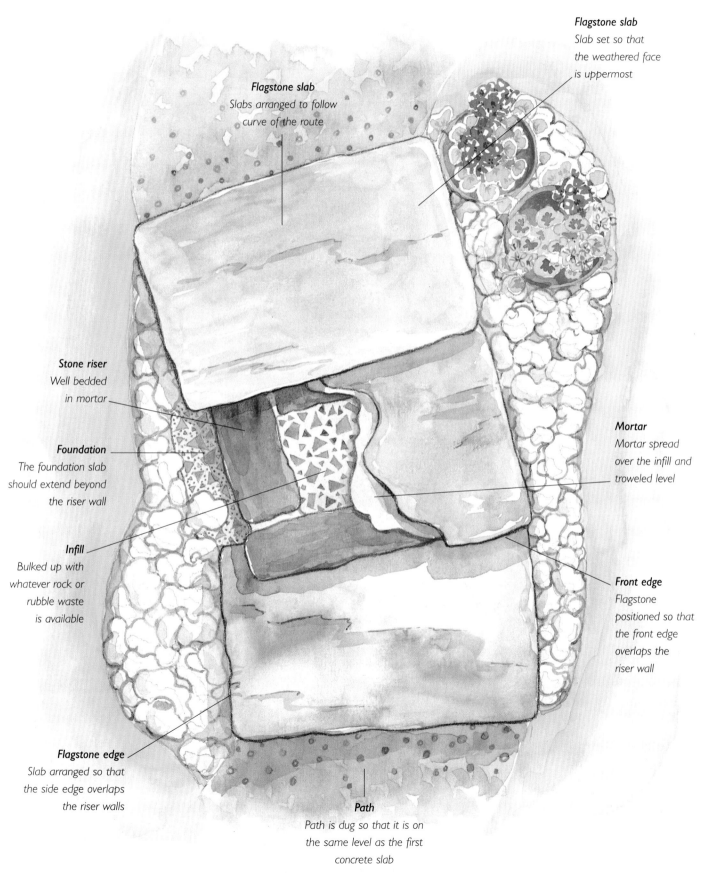

Flagstone slab
Slab set so that
the weathered face
is uppermost

Flagstone slab
Slabs arranged to follow
curve of the route

Stone riser
Well bedded
in mortar

Foundation
The foundation slab
should extend beyond
the riser wall

Infill
Bulked up with
whatever rock or
rubble waste
is available

Mortar
Mortar spread
over the infill and
troweled level

Front edge
Flagstone
positioned so that
the front edge
overlaps the
riser wall

Flagstone edge
Slab arranged so that
the side edge overlaps
the riser walls

Path
Path is dug so that it is on
the same level as the first
concrete slab

Step-by-step: **Making the flagstone steps**

Trench
Cut the trench so that there is room to work

Spoil
Try to minimize the amount of falling earth at this stage

Tamping
Tamp the concrete level with the wooden beam

Marking
Draw around the slab with chalk

Alignment
Angle the flagstone in the direction of the flight

1 To build the first step, mark out the foundation trench with the tape measure, making it about 3 feet (900 mm) wide and 28 inches (700 mm) from front to back. Dig down to a depth of 4 inches (100 mm). Fill the trench with concrete and tamp it down with the wooden beam. Check that it is level.

2 Leave the concrete foundation to harden overnight. Next, place a flagstone on the concrete, angling it in the direction of the flight, and mark the position with the chalk. Put the flagstone to one side.

Corners
Keep the corners crisp and square

Trimming
Trim the stone for the best fit

3 Allowing for the flagstone to overhang at the front and side edges by ⅜–¾ in (10–20 mm), select pieces of limestone for the front and side walls of the riser. Trim them to size with the mason's hammer. Pay special attention to the construction of the front and corners of the riser, and make sure they are square.

Helpful hint

The more time that you spend at the dry run stage – choosing and arranging the stones for best fit and trimming edges to shape – the easier it will be when you come to bedding the stones on the mortar.

4 Build the box by bedding the five courses of split limestone in mortar, building to a height of 5 inches (125 mm). Fill the cavity with concrete and waste stone, tamp down level with the beam, and leave to set. Use the bricklayer's trowel to butter a 1-inch-layer (30 mm) of mortar over the top of the step. Some of the mortar will ooze out when the flagstone is positioned.

Filling
Fill the cavity with concrete and waste stone

Leveling
Tamp the courses level with the beam

Positioning
Slowly lower the flagstone onto the bed of mortar

Horizontal check
Check the foundation with the level

Adjustment
When the slab is in place, adjust it so that the front edge slopes down by ⅜ in (10 mm) so rain can run off

5 Carefully lower the flagstone into position. Tamp it down with the drill hammer and make sure it is level. Adjust the stone so that the front edge slopes down by ⅜ inch (10 mm). Use the pointing trowel to tidy up the mortar.

Tamping
Use the beam to tamp the concrete level

Concrete
The concrete foundation needs to be level with the flagstone

6 To build the next step, dig another foundation cavity (the same size as the first cavity) behind the first step. Fill the cavity, build the riser walls, and position the flagstone as in step 5. Repeat the procedure for each new step.

Alpine hypertufa trough

In the 1940s, gardeners developed a technique for covering old glazed white kitchen sinks with a mixture of sphagnum moss, sand, and cement to make them look like stone. It was called *hypertufa*, after tufa, the rock it resembled, and became all the rage. This project takes the technique one step further in that we cast a whole trough from hypertufa. The project rises up like magic from the ground!

TIME

Two weekends: two days to dig out the mold and for casting (five days for the hypertufa to cure), and two more days for digging out the trough.

SAFETY

This project involves a lot of strenuous digging and heaving – you will need a willing helper.

CROSS-SECTION OF THE TROUGH

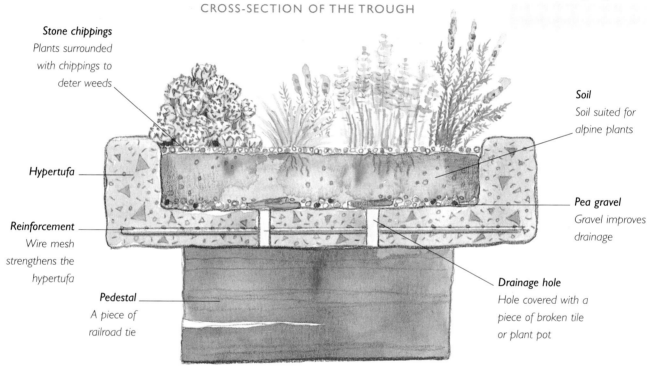

Stone chippings
Plants surrounded with chippings to deter weeds

Hypertufa

Reinforcement
Wire mesh strengthens the hypertufa

Pedestal
A piece of railroad tie

Soil
Soil suited for alpine plants

Pea gravel
Gravel improves drainage

Drainage hole
Hole covered with a piece of broken tile or plant pot

YOU WILL NEED

Materials *for a trough 24 in (600 mm) long, 16 in (400 mm) wide, and 5 in (130 mm) high*
- Hypertufa mix: 50 lb (25 kg) cement, 50 lb (25 kg) sharp sand, 200 lb (100 kg) sphagnum moss
- Broomstick dowels: two 6 in (150 mm) long
- Wire grid mesh: 1 in (25 mm) mesh, 22 in (570 mm) long, 14 in (370 mm) wide
- Railroad tie: 16 in (400 mm) long, 12 in (300 mm) wide, 6 in (145 mm) thick

Tools
- Spade and shovel
- Tape measure
- String line and 8 pegs
- Level and sledgehammer
- Gardening trowel
- Mason's hammer
- Wheelbarrow and bucket
- Wooden tamping beam: about 24 in (600 mm) long, 3 in (80 mm) wide, and 1 in (25 mm) thick
- Wire clippers
- Pointing trowel
- Stiff brush

BURIED TREASURE

Find an area of rough, uncultivated ground in the garden for casting the trough – perhaps a corner of the vegetable plot, or a flower bed that is going to be grassed over. Ideally, you need an area that is reasonably well drained: A mix of heavy loam and clay (where you can squeeze a handful of the earth into a ball that holds its shape) would be perfect. If you study the working drawings and the photographs, you will see that the trough is cast upside down, with a sheet of wire mesh used to reinforce the base. The drainage holes are created by the two dowels. The hollows and bumps in the ground are reversed to become bumps and holes in the trough or, to put it another way, the hollow of the trough starts out as a bump in the ground. The finished trough weighs about 300 pounds (150 kg), which might make it difficult to get out of the ground, so enlist the help of friends and family.

Alpine hypertufa trough

FRONT VIEW OF TROUGH

Rock feature
*Alpine plants growing
on a piece of stone*

Hypertufa trough
*24 x 16 x 5 in
(600 x 400 x
130 mm)*

Wooden pedestal
*A piece of railroad tie,
16 x 12 x 6 in (400
x 300 x 145 mm),
raises the planter
off the ground and
adds contrast*

PLAN VIEW OF TROUGH

Sides of trough
*Casting hypertufa in
earth produces a
rugged, stonelike finish*

Strong sides
*Sides are at least
2¾ in (70 mm) thick*

PLAN VIEW OF TROUGH DURING CASTING

Hypertufa
A final layer – smoothed and leveled – covers the mesh

Reinforcement
Wire mesh is positioned within the thickness of the base

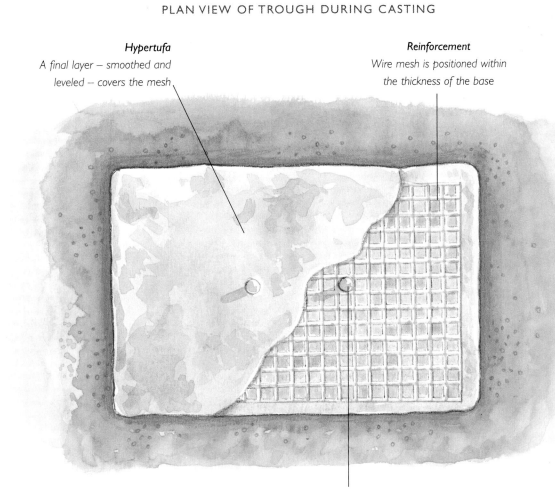

Dowel
Dowel inserted through the mesh and entire thickness of the base (to create drainage holes)

CROSS-SECTION OF TROUGH DURING EXCAVATION

Excavation
A hole is dug around the trough

Hypertufa

Dowel

Reinforcing mesh
Set approximately half-way through the 2 in (50 mm) thickness of the trough base

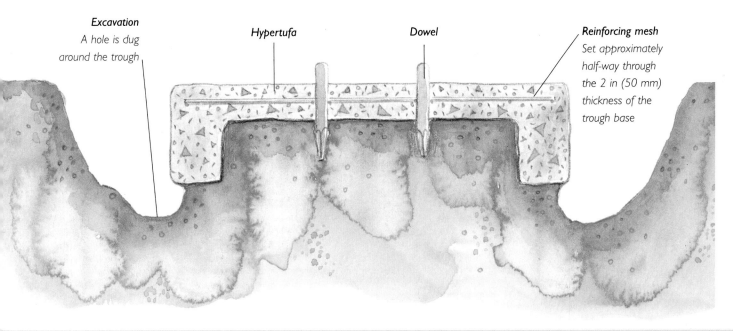

Step-by-step: **Making the alpine hypertufa trough**

Marking out
Set the shape out with pegs and string

Corners
The position of the pegs allows the string to cross over at the corners

1 Clear the ground of weeds and stones and skim it level with a spade. Use the tape measure, string, and pegs to set out a rectangle about 24 inches (600 mm) long and 16 inches (400 mm) wide.

Helpful hint

The traditional method of using two pegs at the corners, with the strings crossing, not only allows you to set out the shape without damaging the earth at the corners, but it also means that you can leave the arrangement in place when you are excavating.

Level
Adjust the level of the earth prior to pounding

Pounding
Pound the earth to a hard, compacted finish

2 Having pegged out the form and checked the overall level with the level, take the sledgehammer and systematically pound the earth around the strings until it is hard and compact.

Scoring
Use the point of the trowel to score a guideline

Digging
Work with small strokes to keep the edges crisp

Depth
Clean out the earth to a depth of 2 in (50 mm)

3 Following the line of the string, score the rectangle on the ground with the gardening trowel. Remove the pegs and string. Excavate the area to a depth of about 2 inches (50 mm). Try to keep the sides of the excavation clean and sharp.

Trench width
The trench needs to be 2¾ in (70 mm) wide

Trench depth
Dig out the trench to a total depth of 5 in (130 mm)

4 Measure in 2¾ inches (70 mm) from the sides of the hole, then sink this area a further 3 inches (80 mm). You should be left with an upside down trough shape with a total depth of 5 inches (130 mm). Bang the two dowels into the central base with the mason's hammer. Mix up the hypertufa by adding water to the cement, sharp sand, and moss. It should resemble cottage cheese.

Dowels
Be careful you do not break up the earth when you hammer in the dowels

Wire mesh
If necessary, trim the mesh to fit over the two pegs

Tamping
Top up the hypertufa so it is level with the ground and tamp down

5 Fill the excavation with hypertufa to within 1 inch (25 mm) of the surface and tamp it level. Cut the mesh with the clippers and fit it over the pegs. Top up the mix to ground level and tamp down. Smooth off with the pointing trowel.

Curing
The water improves the curing process

Holes
The drainage holes run right through the base

Cleaning
Scrub off all traces of earth using a brush

6 Wait about five days for the hypertufa to cure, then carefully excavate the trough. Ease out the two pegs and use a stiff brush and running water to remove all traces of loose earth. Sit the finished trough on the railway sleeper.

Inspirations: Troughs and planters

Nothing beats troughs and planters for versatility in the garden. They can be filled with eye-catching displays at any time of year, giving you the opportunity to make the most of what is in season. Many objects can be used as containers, ranging from a classic lead cistern from a grand house, to a stone drinking trough for animals, an old sink, or a modern reconstituted stone or wooden trough.

ABOVE **A classic trough hosts a flourish of *Helichrysum petiolare*, pelargoniums, and various seedlings. The trough neatly indicates that the door is not in use. The plants have all been left in their pots so that the display can be changed easily.**

RIGHT **A simple stone trough contrasts beautifully with the traditional brickwork of the walls and the bold ceramic pot alongside. The planting themes of the two containers echo each other, visually linking two rather different objects together.**

FAR RIGHT **An ancient stone trough, planted with *Aubretia deltoidea*, mounted on a stone pedestal. It is thought by the owner that both the trough and the base are ecclesiastical — perhaps a font with a piece of broken capital for the base.**

Paved circle

The wonderful thing about a paved circle is that it immediately becomes a focus point in the garden. Children enjoy playing hop, skip and jump games on the pattern of stones, it is a good surface for bench seats and tables, and it makes a really great barbecue area. This design is 8 ft (2.5 m) in diameter, but make it bigger if desired.

TIME

A weekend (about eight hours to remove the lawn and level the ground, and eight hours to lay the slabs).

CAUTION

The slabs are both sharp-edged and fragile, so wear gloves and take care when you are setting them down.

CROSS-SECTION OF HALF OF THE PAVED CIRCLE

Hole depth
Dig out the soil to a depth of 6 in (150 mm)

Large radius paver
Segments arranged so that the joints are staggered

Small radius paver
These are sized to fit inside the large radius pavers

Radius tile unit
Arranged to fit closely around the center

Central circular paver

Radius brick unit
Arranged so that it is slightly higher than the paving but slightly lower than the grass

Sand
Firmly compacted sharp sand, 2½–3 in (70–80 mm) deep

Soil
A well-drained ground is ideal

YOU WILL NEED

Materials for a circle 9 ft 4 in (2.54 m) in diameter
- Central circular paver: 17¾ in (450 mm) in diameter
- Radius tile units: four 9¼ in (235 mm) (inside radius)
- Small radius pavers: sixteen 19 in (485 mm) (inside radius)
- Large radius pavers: sixteen 26½ in (675 mm) (inside radius)
- Radius brick units: sixteen 41 in (1.04 m) (inside radius)

- Sharp sand: 110 lb (50 kg)
- Lime: 110 lb (50 kg)

Tools
- Wheelbarrow
- Tape measure
- String line
- Spade
- Fork
- Rake
- Heavy wooden mallet
- Wooden tamping beam: about 20 in (500 mm) long, 2½ in (60 mm) wide, and 2 in (50 mm) thick
- Level
- Broom

MAGIC CIRCLES

Wander around your garden to work out the best place for a circle that is about 8 ft (2.5 m) in diameter. It could be under a tree, which would make a nice shaded area for a bench seat and table, or in a central position to make a feature, perhaps with a sundial. Study the garden in terms of adequate drainage, shade, sun, and flow of traffic, and assess the pros and cons of the options.

When you have decided on a possible site, make sure that the area is free from underground pipes and drain covers. If you have the plans for your property, pipes may be marked; if not, dig very carefully. Use the string line to scribe a circle to size, and then stand back to see how it fits in with the garden. As a further check, to make sure that you like the position of the circle before committing to construction, set out the slabs and leave them in place for a couple of days. Note how the circle relates to the sun and shade throughout the day. When you are satisfied with the position, chop around the circle with the spade, remove the paving slabs to a safe place, and the work can begin.

Paved circle

PLAN VIEW OF HALF OF THE PAVED CIRCLE

Radius brick level
*The edging is set
slightly lower than the
surrounding grass*

Spacing
*Slab spacing adjusted
until the joints look even*

Levels
*All the radius pavers, radius tile units,
and the central paver are set at the
same level, but slightly lower than that
of the radius bricks*

Dry-mix mortar
*A dry mix of lime and
sand is brushed into
the joints*

Radius tile units
*9¼ in (235 mm) (inside radius)
Segments arranged so that the
radial joints are equally spaced*

Central circular paver
*17¾ in (450 mm) in diameter
Can be shaped, such as a
millstone, or made of bricks*

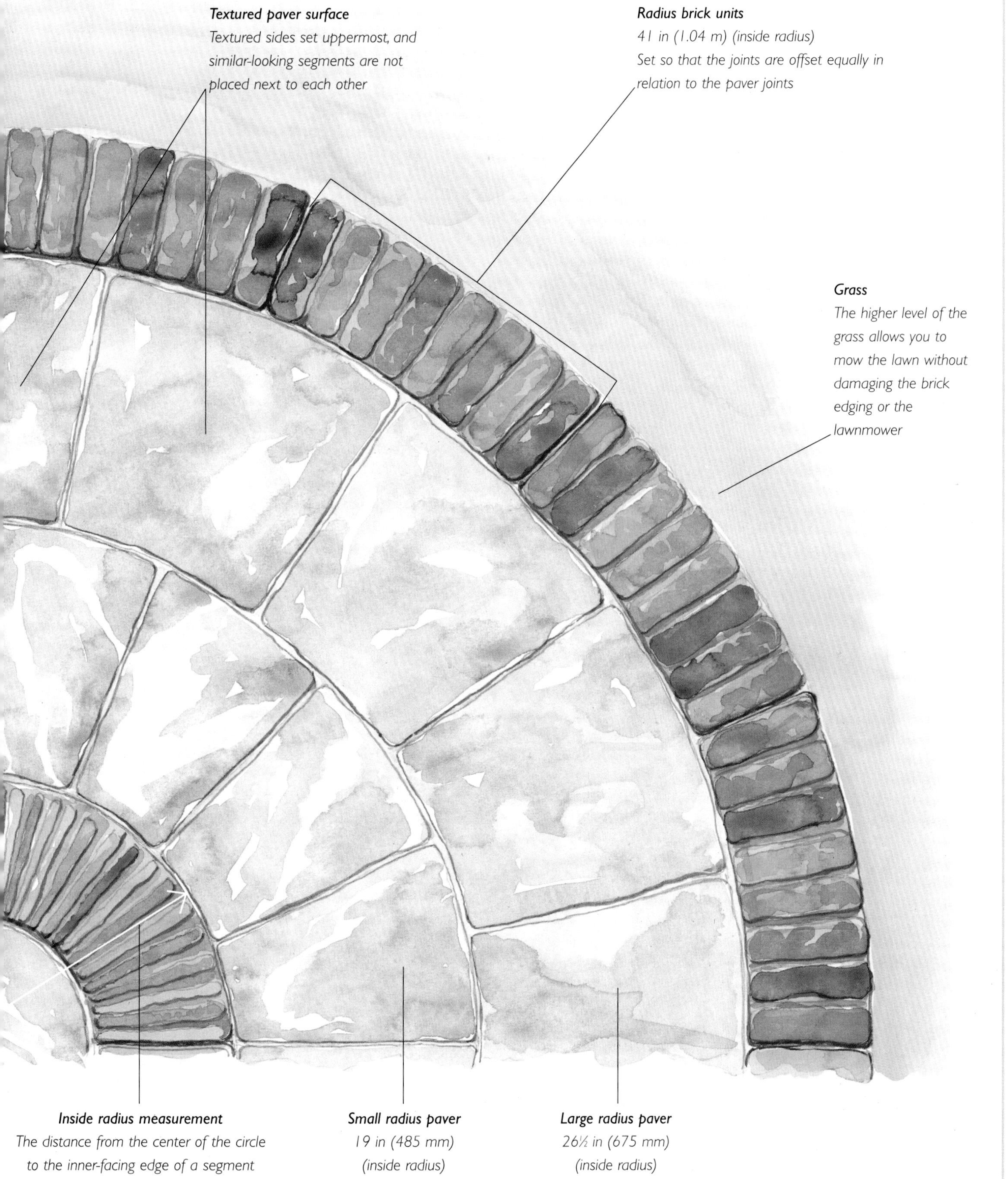

Textured paver surface
Textured sides set uppermost, and similar-looking segments are not placed next to each other

Radius brick units
41 in (1.04 m) (inside radius)
Set so that the joints are offset equally in relation to the paver joints

Grass
The higher level of the grass allows you to mow the lawn without damaging the brick edging or the lawnmower

Inside radius measurement
The distance from the center of the circle to the inner-facing edge of a segment

Small radius paver
19 in (485 mm)
(inside radius)

Large radius paver
26½ in (675 mm)
(inside radius)

Step-by-step: **Making the paved circle**

Earth
Dig out the earth to a depth of 6 in (150 mm)

Circle center
The intersection of the arcs marks the center

Stones
Remove any rubble and big stones

Raking
Rake the sand level and smooth

Compacting
Do not worry about walking on the sand

1 Use the spade and fork to remove all the sod and earth from the marked area down to a depth of about 6 inches (150 mm), then rake the earth level. Cover the area with a layer of sand to a depth of 2½–3 inches (70–80 mm) and rake it smooth and level.

2 To find the center of the circle, use the string line. Set it to measure the radius of the circle, then drag the line at a couple of points around the circumference and draw arcs. The intersection of the arcs is the center of the circle.

Tamping
Hit the beam with the mallet rather than hitting the slab

3 Put the circular slab at the center and tamp it in place with the mallet and wooden beam. Check with the level and make corrections until the slab lies absolutely level.

Horizontal check
Make sure the slab is positioned correctly using the level

Leveling
You might need to pack sand under the slab to adjust the level

Segments
Handle fragile segments with great care

Packing
A dipped slab needs to be raised with extra sand underneath

4 Working outwards from the center, carefully position the other slabs (the circle of radius tile units, the circle of small radius pavers, and so on), all the while checking with the level and correcting any dips and hollows with extra sand.

Helpful hint

If you experience difficulties when you come to spacing the slabs, finding joints either too wide or too tight, use pieces of hardboard or plywood, ⅜–½ in (10–15 mm) thick, as spacers. Insert them between the slabs to gauge the distance.

Joints
Continue brushing until the joints are filled and level

Staggered joints
Make sure that the segments are centered with adjacent joints

5 Make sure, when you come to fitting the radius brick units, that the joints are staggered with the large radius pavers.

Broom
Use a stiff broom to move the mortar mix around

6 Finally, shovel the dry-mix mortar (a mixture of 2 parts sand to 1 part lime) over the slabs. Use the broom to spread and sweep it evenly into all the joints. Spray water over the whole circle.

Multicolored crazy paving path

This path draws its inspiration from the hard colors and cool curves of the 1950s. It is relatively cheap to make, and will inject retro zing into any garden. You can choose the color selection according to your personal artistic vision.

TIME

A weekend (about eight hours to prepare the site and fit the curbstones, and eight hours to lay the slabs).

SAFETY

Slabs sometimes spit out splinters when being broken, so wear goggles if you have to trim any.

YOU WILL NEED

Materials *for a path 15 ft (4.5 m) long and 40 in (1 m) wide*
- Concrete "York stone" blocks: 20 blocks, 9¾ in (450 mm) long, 6 in (150 mm) wide and 2½ in (65 mm) thick
- Broken concrete paving slabs: about 5 square yards (meters)
- Concrete: 1 part (94 lb or 50 kg) cement, 2 parts (200 lb or 100 kg) sharp sand, 3 parts (300 lb or 150 kg) aggregate
- Gravel: 1 ton medium-sized (pea) gravel
- Sharp sand: 1 ton
For the dry-mix mortar:
- Lime: 50 lb (25 kg)

- Cement: 50 lb (25 kg)
- Sand: 200 lb (100 kg) (taken from the ton of sharp sand)

Tools
- Wooden pegs and string line
- Wheelbarrow
- Spade
- Bricklayer's trowel
- Mason's hammer
- Shovel
- Rake
- Level
- Walking board: about 3 ft (900 mm) long, 1 ft (300 mm) wide, and 1 in (30 mm) thick
- Sledgehammer
- Broom

COOL, CRAZY COLORS

The good thing about a crazy paving path is that it can be as wide and curvy as you like, because it doesn't have to conform to the limitations of a particular size of slab. If you have a fancy for a path that snakes around the beds and borders, crazy paving is a good option. Better still, the pieces of broken concrete slab are cheap, so you get a longer path for your money.

Consider how a path might complement the shape of your garden. Visit manufacturers and builder's suppliers to look at the available slabs. Some slabs are smooth on one side and heavily textured on the other, with the color running through the thickness, while others are smooth on both sides and have only one colored face. When you have made your selection, play around with the broken pieces to see how they might fit together to create an overall uniformity. Plan out the route of the path and mark the edges with pegs and string. Clear the ground down to a depth of 6 inches (150 mm), making it 40 inches (1 m) wide. Dig a trench at either side of it, 10 inches (250 mm) wide and with a total depth of 10 inches (250 mm).

CROSS-SECTION ACROSS THE WIDTH OF THE PATH

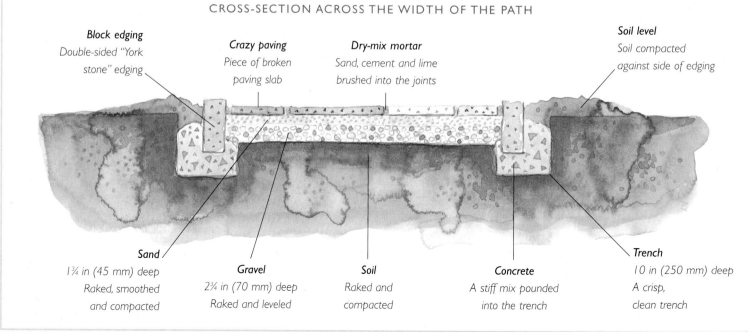

Block edging
Double-sided "York stone" edging

Crazy paving
Piece of broken paving slab

Dry-mix mortar
Sand, cement and lime brushed into the joints

Soil level
Soil compacted against side of edging

Sand
1¾ in (45 mm) deep Raked, smoothed and compacted

Gravel
2¾ in (70 mm) deep Raked and leveled

Soil
Raked and compacted

Concrete
A stiff mix pounded into the trench

Trench
10 in (250 mm) deep A crisp, clean trench

Multicolored crazy paving path

PLAN VIEW OF THE PATH

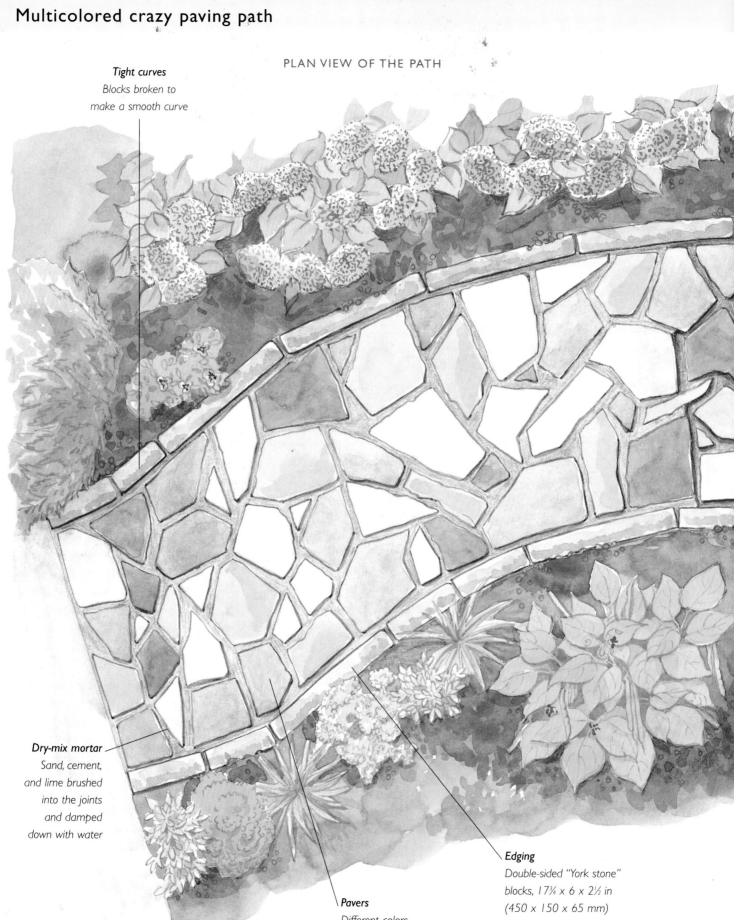

Tight curves
*Blocks broken to
make a smooth curve*

Dry-mix mortar
*Sand, cement,
and lime brushed
into the joints
and damped
down with water*

Pavers
*Different colors
distributed evenly*

Edging
*Double-sided "York stone"
blocks, 17¾ x 6 x 2½ in
(450 x 150 x 65 mm)*

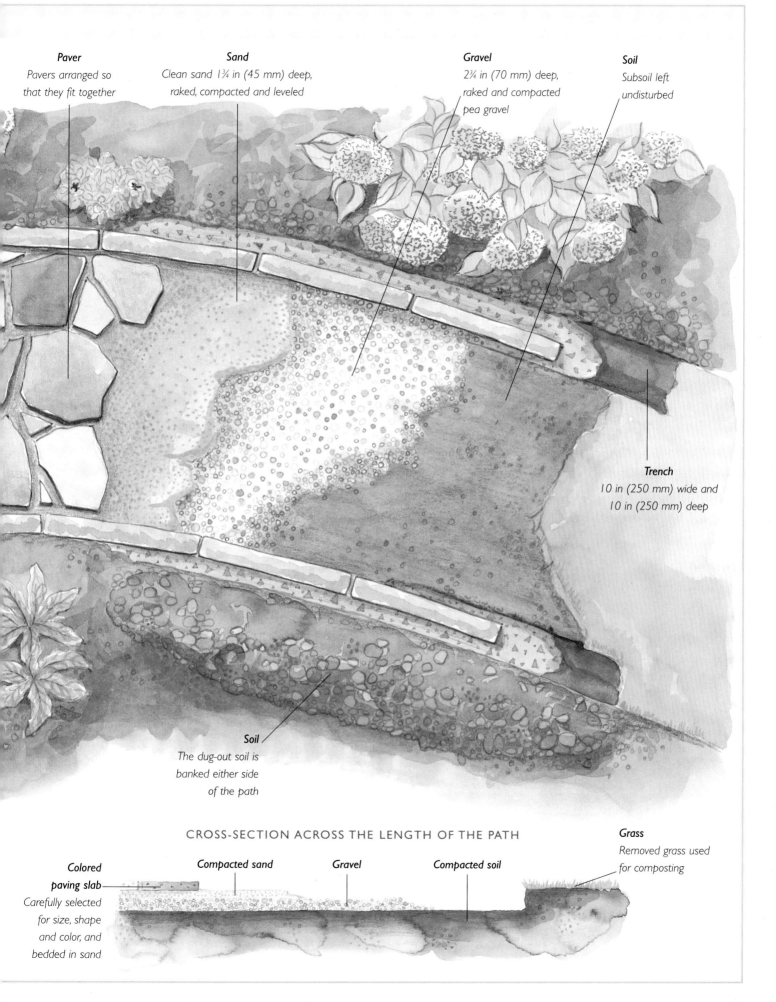

Paver
Pavers arranged so
that they fit together

Sand
Clean sand 1¾ in (45 mm) deep,
raked, compacted and leveled

Gravel
2¾ in (70 mm) deep,
raked and compacted
pea gravel

Soil
Subsoil left
undisturbed

Trench
10 in (250 mm) wide and
10 in (250 mm) deep

Soil
The dug-out soil is
banked either side
of the path

CROSS-SECTION ACROSS THE LENGTH OF THE PATH

**Colored
paving slab**
Carefully selected
for size, shape
and color, and
bedded in sand

Compacted sand

Gravel

Compacted soil

Grass
Removed grass used
for composting

Step-by-step: Making the multicolored crazy paving path

Concrete
Be generous with the amount of concrete

Raking
Rake the gravel to a depth of 2¾ in (70 mm)

Leveling
Use the trowel handle to nudge the blocks into position

Cavity
Push the gravel right into the curb trench

Compacting
Firm up the gravel with your feet

1 Fill the two trenches with concrete, up to the base level of the path. Carefully set the concrete edging blocks in place to make the curb. With the bricklayer's trowel and mason's hammer, adjust the blocks so that three-quarters of the block rises above the path base.

2 Shovel the gravel over the earth in the path area and rake it to a depth of 2¾ in (70 mm). Push it into the cavity alongside the edging blocks, and generally rake it so that it follows the level of the ground. Use the level to see whether it is true, and even out by raking if necessary.

Sand level
Keep the sand 1½ in (35 mm) below the curb stones

Sand depth
Aim for a depth of 1¾ in (45 mm)

3 Cover the gravel with a layer of sand to a depth of about 1¾ in (45 mm). Rake it level and stamp it down so that the surface is about 1½ in (35 mm) lower than the top of the curb. Check that it is level with the level.

Helpful hint

It's always a good idea, when ordering sand and gravel, to specify "well washed." This will minimize the chances of the sand and gravel being contaminated with clay or salt. You cannot use salty sand in concrete or mortar mixes, because it will damage it.

Spacing
Leave a gap of 1 in
(25 mm) between the pavers

4 Set the pieces of broken slab into place on the sand, leaving about 1 in (25 mm) between them. Try and position the pieces so that there is a good spread of the various colors.

Laying the slabs
Bed the slabs into the sand

Colors
Aim for an even spread of colors

Walking board
Stand on the board so that you do not dislodge the slabs

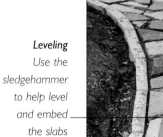

Leveling
Use the sledgehammer to help level and embed the slabs

5 Put the walking board on the path and use your weight and the sledgehammer to thump the slabs into place, so that they sit firmly in the sand.

Brushing
Move the dry-mix mortar around with a broom

Dry-mix mortar
Make sure the cement, sand and lime are well blended

6 Make a dry-mix mortar of 4 parts sand, 1 part cement, and 1 part lime, and sweep it over the path with the broom, so that it falls into all the cracks. Spray with water. Leave for 24 hours.

Tranquil Japanese garden

What better way of creating an area of calm, reflection and tranquility, than to build a traditional Japanese garden? It's a beautiful, simple concept that involves gathering a number of basic elements – a traditional lantern, natural rocks and crushed stone – and then carefully arranging them to form a three-dimensional picture.

TIME

Two weekends (about eight hours to build the frame and level the site, sixteen hours to build the lantern, and eight hours to assemble the whole thing).

SAFETY

Building the lantern involves moving a number of back-breaking lumps of stone, so use a hand truck and get someone to help you.

YOU WILL NEED

Materials *for a garden 8 ft (2.4 m) square*
- Wooden beams: 4 treated posts, 8 ft (2.4 m) long, 4 in (100 mm) wide, and 4 in (100 mm) thick
- Pegs: 4 pieces of scrap wood, about 1 in (25 mm) square and 6 in (150 mm) long
- Woven plastic sheet, 8 ft (2.4 m) square
- Gravel: 1000 lb (500 kg) washed gravel
- Boulders: 3 large limestone rocks
- Split sandstone: 4 or 5 large slices of stone
- Mortar: 2 parts (44 lb or 20 kg) cement, 1 part (22 lb or 10 kg) lime, 9 parts (200 lb or 90 kg) soft sand
- Oyster shell grit: 200 lb (100 kg) washed grit
- Lantern base: block of salvaged weathered cut limestone, about 15 in (380 mm) square and 5½ in (140 mm) thick
- Lantern column: block of salvaged weathered cut limestone, 28 in (700 mm) long, 12 in (300 mm) wide, and 5 in (130 mm) thick
- Lantern table: slab of salvaged weathered cut limestone, 12 in (300 mm) square and 4¼ in (110 mm) thick
- Lantern pillars: slab of salvaged weathered cut limestone, 9½ in (240 mm) long, 7 in (180 mm) wide, and 2 in (50 mm) thick
- Lantern roof: slab of salvaged weathered cut limestone, 12 in (300 mm) square and 2 in (50 mm) thick
- Roof finial: slab of salvaged weathered cut limestone, 6 in (150 mm) square and 2 in (50 mm) thick
- Finial cobble: a large feature stone, about 4 in (100 mm) in diameter

Tools
- Tape measure, square, chalk
- Crosscut saw
- Mallet and 1 in (25 mm)-wide woodworking chisel
- Electric drill fitted with a 1 in (25 mm)-diameter woodworking drill bit
- Bucket and shovel
- Rake and fork
- Pointing trowel
- Level
- Electric angle grinder with a stone-cutting disc

THE WORLD IN STONE

Think of the items in a Japanese garden as being elements that symbolize our physical and spiritual world – stones are mountains, raked grit is flowing water, large stones are guardians, stone lanterns light our path, and so on. The whole idea is to create a three-dimensional picture of the world. First you build the frame, then "paint" the scene with the stones.

The stone lantern is made from carefully selected pieces of salvaged stone. The four little pillars that support the lantern roof slab are made up of briquettes. These are cut by a simple procedure that involves using an angle grinder to score lines part-way through a limestone slab, first on one side and then on the other, before snapping the slab. The sides of the briquettes reveal a beautiful texture, the result of a machined face and a natural break. The secret of creating a really stunning lantern is to obtain stones with character – visit an architectural salvage company for the best choice, and spend time making your selection.

CROSS-SECTION OF THE JAPANESE GARDEN

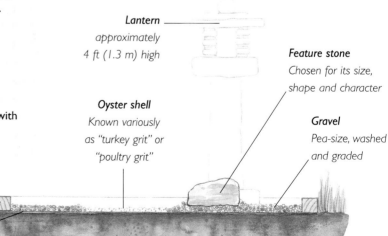

Lantern
approximately
4 ft (1.3 m) high

Feature stone
Chosen for its size,
shape and character

Oyster shell
Known variously
as "turkey grit" or
"poultry grit"

Gravel
Pea-size, washed
and graded

Wooden frame

Plastic sheet

Tranquil Japanese garden

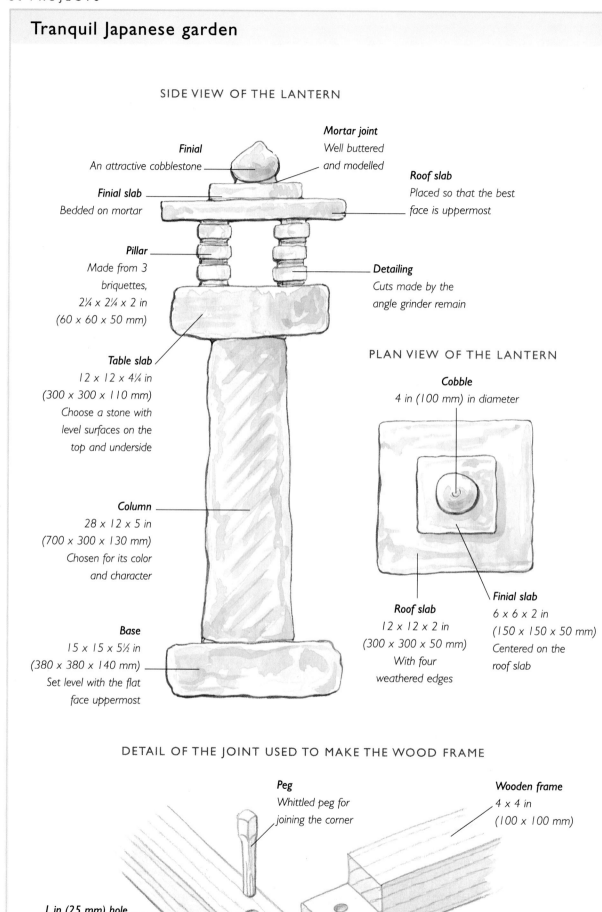

SIDE VIEW OF THE LANTERN

Finial
An attractive cobblestone

Mortar joint
Well buttered
and modelled

Roof slab
Placed so that the best
face is uppermost

Finial slab
Bedded on mortar

Pillar
Made from 3
briquettes,
2¼ x 2¼ x 2 in
(60 x 60 x 50 mm)

Detailing
Cuts made by the
angle grinder remain

Table slab
12 x 12 x 4¼ in
(300 x 300 x 110 mm)
Choose a stone with
level surfaces on the
top and underside

Column
28 x 12 x 5 in
(700 x 300 x 130 mm)
Chosen for its color
and character

Base
15 x 15 x 5½ in
(380 x 380 x 140 mm)
Set level with the flat
face uppermost

PLAN VIEW OF THE LANTERN

Cobble
4 in (100 mm) in diameter

Roof slab
12 x 12 x 2 in
(300 x 300 x 50 mm)
With four
weathered edges

Finial slab
6 x 6 x 2 in
(150 x 150 x 50 mm)
Centered on the
roof slab

DETAIL OF THE JOINT USED TO MAKE THE WOOD FRAME

Peg
Whittled peg for
joining the corner

Wooden frame
4 x 4 in
(100 x 100 mm)

I in (25 mm) hole
To take peg

Joint
Notch sawn out,
4 x 2 in (100 x 50 mm)

PLAN VIEW OF THE GARDEN

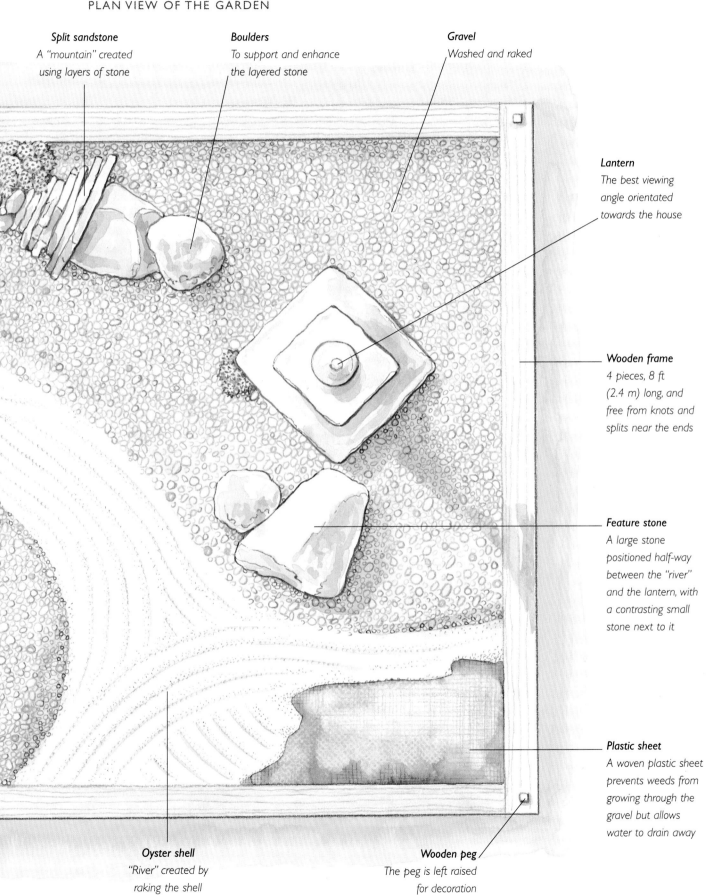

Split sandstone
A "mountain" created
using layers of stone

Boulders
To support and enhance
the layered stone

Gravel
Washed and raked

Lantern
The best viewing
angle orientated
towards the house

Wooden frame
4 pieces, 8 ft
(2.4 m) long, and
free from knots and
splits near the ends

Feature stone
A large stone
positioned half-way
between the "river"
and the lantern, with
a contrasting small
stone next to it

Plastic sheet
A woven plastic sheet
prevents weeds from
growing through the
gravel but allows
water to drain away

Oyster shell
"River" created by
raking the shell

Wooden peg
The peg is left raised
for decoration

Step-by-step: **Making the tranquil Japanese garden**

Gravel
Make sure that the gravel has been washed and is free from salt

Shovel
Use the shovel to spread out the gravel

1 Construct the wooden frame. Draw it out using the tape measure, square and chalk. Remove the waste with the crosscut saw, mallet and chisel. Drill holes as shown in the illustration on page **84**. Use the chisel to whittle the pegs out of scrap wood, and put the frame together. Position it in the garden. Cover the ground inside it with the plastic sheet, tucking the edges under the frame. Shovel the gravel over it.

Stone
Use the stones to build a miniature mountain

Fork
A fork is the best tool for raking the shell

River
Leave a channel through the gravel for making the "river" feature

Oyster shell
Obtained as grit from poultry suppliers

Making waves
Drag the fork to make a ridge and furrow pattern

2 Start placing the symbolic features. Rake the gravel into mounds to make areas of "high ground", then carefully position the boulders and sandstone slabs to create "mountains" and "hills".

3 Decide which area of the garden is to be "water", then spread a thick layer of crushed oyster shell over it. Rake the shell with the prongs of the fork to create "ripples" and "waves".

Column
*Make sure the lantern
column is vertical*

4 Position the base block of the lantern. Butter the base of the column stone with mortar, using the pointing trowel. Set the column in place. Check that it is vertical with the level and then leave until the mortar has stiffened. Butter the top of the column with mortar, and lower the lantern table into position.

Helpful hint

The best you can do when testing a rugged piece of stone with a level is to aim for what was traditionally known as "best fit" — meaning you take readings from all sides and make a judgment.

Wedging
*You may need
to use small
pieces of
stone to wedge
the column*

Pillars
Tap the blocks straight

Finial slab
*Carefully set the finial
slab in place*

Mortar
*Butter the
blocks with
the mortar*

5 Set out the dimensions of the briquettes with the tape measure and chalk, and use the angle grinder to cut them out. Butter them with mortar and build the little pillars. Tap down with the trowel handle to adjust the levels.

Mortar
*Butter the
roof slab
with mortar*

Roof slab
*Make sure the
slab is well
bedded on to
the pillars*

6 Spread mortar on top of the four pillars. Place the roof slab on the pillars, and butter it with mortar. Carefully position the finial slab. Set the feature cobble in place, fixing it with mortar that is modeled to fit the contours of the stone.

Dry-stone retaining wall

Crisscrossing hill and dale, dry-stone walls are the traditional way of controlling livestock and marking boundaries. The technique evolved over many thousands of years. It does not require cement or mortar – just stone upon stone to create a beautiful structure that is uniquely capable of withstanding the weather.

TIME

A weekend (two days to build a wall about 16 ft [4.8 m] long and 5½ ft [800 mm] high).

SPECIAL TIPS

Since trucking costs for transporting stones are so high, it is best to be over-generous when estimating quantities. If in doubt, seek advice from your supplier.

YOU WILL NEED

Materials *for a wall 16 ft (4.8 m) long and 5½ ft (800 mm) high*
- Split stone (sandstone or limestone): 1.5 tons
- Hardcore for the foundation (either waste stone or builder's rubble): 5 wheelbarrow loads
- Keystone: attractive heavy stone, about 1 ft (300 mm) long, 8 in (200 mm) wide, and 8 in (200 mm) thick

Tools
- Wheelbarrow
- Spade and shovel
- Tape measure
- String line
- Drill hammer
- Bolster chisel
- Piece of old carpet
- Bricklayer's trowel
- Level
- Rake

A PERFECT PATTERN OF STONE

This wall stands about 5½ feet (800 mm) high for three-quarters of its length, then runs in a gentle curve down to meet the ground. Study your site and work out the total length of the wall that you intend to build. Reckon on ordering about 1 ton of stone for every 10-feet (3-metre) length of wall (you will also need about 3 wheelbarrow loads of hardcore). It's a good idea to add on about ten per cent extra for good measure. When you visit the stoneyard, select split stone about 1–4 inches (30–100 mm) thick, with a flat top and bottom, and a reasonably straight face edge. Choose a firm stone, rather than a stone that crumbles and flakes to the touch. Select rougher, character stones for the coping, such as pieces of weathered stone (maybe even large lumps, rather than slices). Don't forget that you will need hardcore for the foundation trench – this project uses waste stone, but you could also use broken brick, a mixture of gravel and clay, pulverized concrete or whatever else is available.

CROSS-SECTION DETAIL OF THE DRY-STONE WALL

Coping
A line of stones, on edge, to finish the wall

Stone
Split sandstone, limestone or broken pavers

Plants
Plants to reinforce the coping

Earth
The earth is retained by the wall

Tie stones
The occasional use of long stones provides extra stability, tying the wall to the earth

Stone chips
Small pieces of stone used to maintain level

Earth
Firmed up against the base of the wall

Foundation
Compacted rubble

Dry-stone retaining wall

PLAN VIEW OF THE WALL

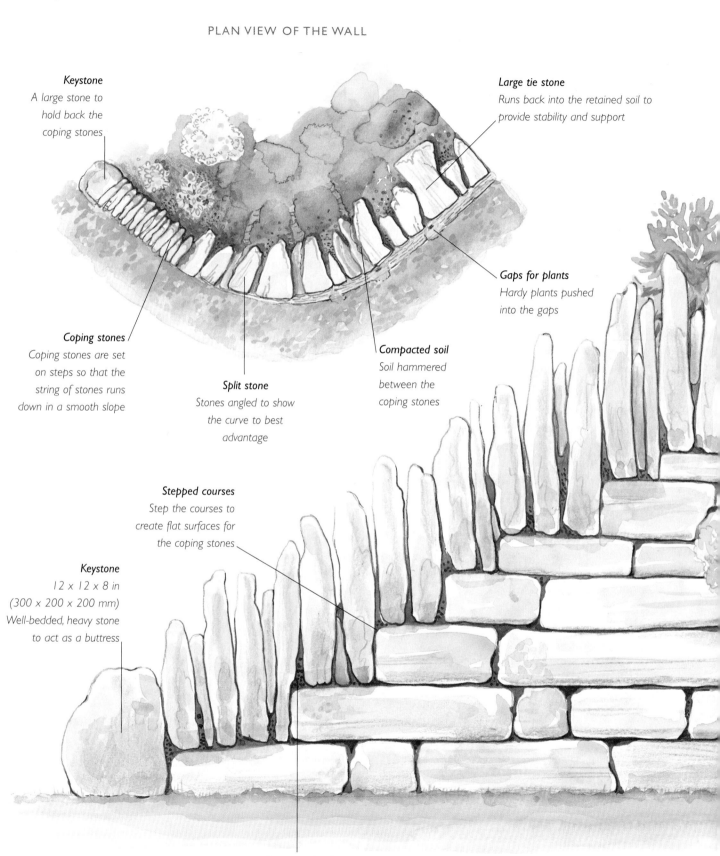

Keystone
A large stone to
hold back the
coping stones

Large tie stone
Runs back into the retained soil to
provide stability and support

Coping stones
Coping stones are set
on steps so that the
string of stones runs
down in a smooth slope

Gaps for plants
Hardy plants pushed
into the gaps

Split stone
Stones angled to show
the curve to best
advantage

Compacted soil
Soil hammered
between the
coping stones

Stepped courses
Step the courses to
create flat surfaces for
the coping stones

Keystone
12 x 12 x 8 in
(300 x 200 x 200 mm)
Well-bedded, heavy stone
to act as a buttress

Compacted soil
Soil pounded into
the cavities

SIDE VIEW OF THE WALL

Thin slices and chips
Used to bring the course up to a common level

Small stones
Use small pieces to wedge larger stones

Coping
12 in (300 mm) high Arranged so that the best edge is facing forward

Small infill
A small but long stone wedged to fill a gap

Gaps for plants
The plant roots strengthen the wall

Narrow courses
Thinner stones used for contrasting courses

Step-by-step: Making the dry-stone retaining wall

Earth bank
Slope the bank so it does not fall into the trench

Drill hammer
Use a medium-weight drill hammer

Hardcore
Pound the hardcore with the drill hammer to make a solid foundation. Level it off with earth

Carpet
Place carpet underneath the stone

Protection
Wear strong gloves to protect your hands

1 Dig away the earth to reveal the bank of earth that needs retaining. Mark out a trench about 12 in (300 mm) wide and 8 in (200 mm) deep with the string line and tape measure, then excavate it and fill it with compacted hardcore. Level it with earth.

2 Use the drill hammer and the bolster chisel to cut your stock of stone into reasonably-sized pieces. Support the stone on the carpet, set the chisel squarely on top, and then strike the chisel with a single, well-placed blow.

Tamping
Use the wooden handle to align the stones

3 Lay the first row of stones on the leveled foundation, and use the bricklayer's trowel to rake earth down from the bank to support the row. Lay another row, rake down some more earth, and so on. Use the drill hammer to compact the supporting earth and to tamp individual stones into place. Leave hand-sized spaces now and again to form planting pockets.

Bank of earth
Rake the earth down to the level of each stone

Coursing
*Adjust the stones so
that they are all level*

4 At staggered intervals along the rows – say about every yard – carefully select long "tie" stones, and place them so that they run back into the bank. Beat the earth into place around the stones. Check that everything is level with the level.

"Tie" stone
*Run the stone
into the bank
and secure it
with earth*

Helpful hint

Select the long "tie" stones with care. Go for stones that are slightly broader and thicker at the back end – so that most of the weight is anchored into the bank. This helps to give the wall greater stability.

Wedging
*Use small stones to
wedge the coping stones*

Slivers
*Insert slivers of stone to
adjust the coursing level*

Coping stones
*Select character
stones for the
coping course*

Cavities
*Gaps between
the stones
can be filled
with sod*

Sighting
*Look down the
wall to spot
stones that
require tapping
into line*

5 When you have a good wall, wet the surrounding earth and rake it over the top course. Press a row of vertical coping stones into the mud to top off the wall. Rake earth up and between the coping stones, and pound into place.

6 Sight down the finished wall, bang earth into cavities, and tap misfit stones back into line. Adjust individual stones by banging small slivers of waste stone into the cavities.

Inspirations: Dry stone

While wood and wire fences can be intimidating and visually intrusive, and hedges need a lot of upkeep, dry-stone walls melt into the landscape and require the minimum of maintenance. A well-built dry-stone wall can, at one and the same time, protect, exclude, retain, suggest stability, or simply guide the eye from one part of the garden to another. A dry-stone wall or sculpture speaks of permanence.

ABOVE Slate setts used in a new path. The technique of setting slate on edge is common in Cornwall, England, and seen in cottages, quays and churches.

ABOVE A traditional old dry-stone wall in North Devon, England, made from local fieldstone. Ivy-leaved toadflax has colonized the nooks and crannies. The wall is superbly crafted, and the color and texture of the stone harmonize perfectly with the location.

LEFT A monolithic decorative sculpture made using the dry-stone wall technique. The piece stands about 2 yards (meters) high, with each piece of stone running back to the vertical center-line.

Cantilevered seat-shelf

If you would like to build something that uses a massive stone slab and not much else, and you have a good solid wall in your garden, then a cantilevered seat-shelf is a really great idea. The seat looks like it is floating on air!

TIME
A weekend to build (eight hours for fixing the iron support bars, and eight hours for shaping the copper sleeves and placing the stone).

SAFETY
Working with the resin capsules is potentially dangerous, so follow the manufacturer's directions very carefully.

YOU WILL NEED

Materials *for a seat-shelf 4 ft (1.3 m) (or up to 6 ft [2 m]) long and 16 in (400 mm) wide*
- Sill stone: a single salvaged sill stone, 4 ft (1.3 m) to 6 ft (2 m) long, 16 in (400 mm) wide and 2 in (50 mm) thick
- Iron reinforcing bar: 80 in (2 m) long and ¾ in (20 mm) in diameter
- Anchor resin capsules: 3 epoxy acrylate resin capsules, ¾ in (20 mm) in diameter, suitable for fixing metal to stone
- Copper pipe (as used by plumbers): three 22 in (550 mm) long, 1 in (25 mm) in diameter

Tools
- Tape measure and piece of chalk
- Large-size angle grinder with cutting discs for metal and stone
- Electric jack-hammer drill fitted with a 1 in (25 mm) masonry bit (long enough to drill a hole 8 in [200 mm] deep)
- Mason's hammer
- Level
- A short length of railroad tie
- Claw hammer

FLOATING ON AIR

Though this might appear to be a very simple project – no more than a stone slab suspended on cantilevered bars – a lot of work goes into its creation. But if the idea of working with a giant-size drill and a massive angle grinder appeals to you, you will find it fun. The seat-shelf must be sited against a wall at least 10 inches (250 mm) thick, made from solid brick, concrete block, or stone (either the wall of your house, or, better still, a freestanding wall in the garden). The iron reinforcing rods are glued into place by means of anchor resin capsules (sealed glass tubes filled with epoxy resin, a hardener, and granules of stone). The glass tube is eased down the drilled hole, and the iron bar is hammered and twisted into place – the glass breaks, the chemicals mix and cure, and the bar is glued into place. The finished seat-shelf will hold three people, or their equivalent weight in plant pots!

PLAN VIEW OF THE SEAT-SHELF

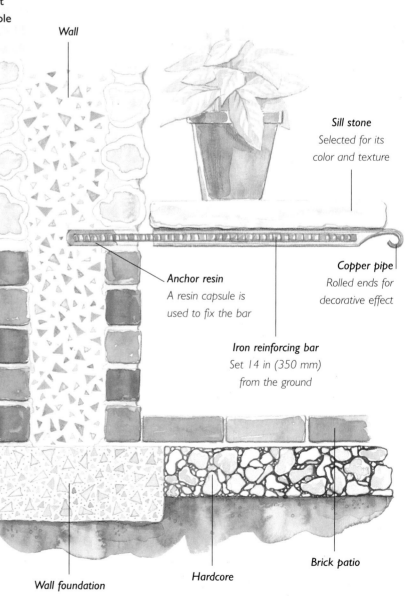

Wall

Sill stone
Selected for its color and texture

Anchor resin
A resin capsule is used to fix the bar

Copper pipe
Rolled ends for decorative effect

Iron reinforcing bar
Set 14 in (350 mm) from the ground

Brick patio

Wall foundation

Hardcore

Cantilevered seat-shelf

FRONT VIEW AND PLAN VIEW OF SEAT SHELF

No attaching needed
*The weight of the sill
stone holds it in place*

Sill stone
*4 to 6 ft x 16 in x 2 in
(1.3 to 2 m x 400
x 50 mm)
Arranged so that the
weathered (textured)
edge faces forwards*

Copper pipe
*Rolled end projects
from under the sill*

Sill stone
*The textured side
faces upwards*

Wall
The wall must be thick and strong

Copper pipe
Flattened, with rolled end

Overhang
The stone must not extend more than 8 in (200 mm) beyond the supporting bar

Reinforcing bar
Supporting bars spaced apart equally, ensuring that the bars are level and aligned with each other

Copper pipe
The pipe slides over the reinforcing bar

Step-by-step: **Making the cantilevered seat-shelf**

Grinder shield
Always have the shield in place

Protection
Wear gloves, goggles and a dust-mask

Grinder angle
Keep the disc at right angles to the stone

Metal cutting
Use a disc designed for cutting metal

Iron bar
Stand on the bar so that it stays still

1 Mark out the sill stone to size. Fit the angle grinder with the stone-cutting disc and trim the back edge of the stone slab to a square finish, so that it measures precisely 16 in (400 mm) wide. Leave the weathered front and side edges intact.

2 Change the disc to the one for cutting metal and cut the iron bar into four lengths – three at 22 in (550 mm) and one at 14 in (350 mm). Make sure your feet are well away from the line of cut.

Hole position
Avoid drilling very hard stones such as granite

3 With the drill, run three holes, 8 in (200 mm) deep, into the wall. These should be level, 14 in (350 mm) up from the ground and about 20 in (500 mm) apart.

Level
All three holes must be level with each other

Drill
Large, powerful drills can be rented from a tool rental shop

Loading the hole
Clear out any dust and push the capsule to the end of the hole

4 Slide an anchor capsule into a hole, follow it up with one of the long iron bars, and then hammer the bar with the mason's hammer to break the glass of the capsule. Make sure that the bar is in the correct position and square to the wall, using the level, then leave it until the resin has set.

Helpful hint

Even though you are wearing goggles, make sure, when you come to breaking the glass capsule, that you stand well to one side – so that you are out of the firing line if the resin squirts out of the hole.

Resin capsules
Handle the capsules with great care

Copper pipe
Bang the flattened pipe end around the iron bar

Level
Make sure the three bars are level with each other

Railroad tie
Use the tie to hold the iron bar

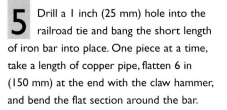

Bar
The bar must be set at right angles to the wall

Copper
The cut end of the pipe should touch the wall

5 Drill a 1 inch (25 mm) hole into the railroad tie and bang the short length of iron bar into place. One piece at a time, take a length of copper pipe, flatten 6 in (150 mm) at the end with the claw hammer, and bend the flat section around the bar.

6 Finally, slide the copper sleeves over the iron bars, check with the level to ensure all is level, and lift the slab into position. Its weight holds it in place.

Sundial

The classic garden sundial must surely be one of the most useful and interesting items to have in the garden. What better way of passing a hot and lazy summer's day than to lounge in the garden and watch as the sundial's shadowy finger slowly but surely marks off the hours? This design fits on an existing patio or other surface.

TIME

A weekend (eight hours to build the base and the column, and eight hours to complete the structure and fit the dial).

SAFETY

Breaking slate is a splintery business, so wear protective goggles.

YOU WILL NEED

Materials *for a sundial 25 in (640 mm) high and 16 in (400 mm) square*

• Mortar: 2 parts (44 lb or 20 kg) cement, 1 part (22 lb or 10 kg) lime, 9 parts (200 lb or 90 kg) soft sand
• Flagstone for the base: a salvaged stone about 16 in (400 mm) square and 3 in (80 mm) thick
• Flagstone for the table: a salvaged stone about 12 in (300 mm) square and 2¼ in (60 mm) thick
• Split slate: 100 lb (50 kg) of broken pieces
• Split sandstone: 100 lb (50 kg) of broken pieces

• A brass sundial of your choice
• Screws and plugs to fit the holes in the brass plate

Tools
• Wheelbarrow
• Bucket
• Tape measure and piece of chalk
• Pointing trowel
• Level
• Mason's hammer
• Drill fitted with a masonry bit (size to match holes in sundial plate)
• Screwdriver to fit the screws

A SUNNY WAY TO PASS THE TIME

When deciding where to put the sundial, you not only have to consider how the structure relates to the design of the garden, but the position must also be one that gets sufficient sunshine in order for the sundial to work. If your garden is mostly surrounded by tall trees, settle for a position that gets the best of the sunshine when you are most likely to be resting in the garden – maybe after lunch, or late in the afternoon.

The structure is made up of four elements – a flagstone slab for the base, a plinth built up from pieces of sandstone, a cylindrical column constructed from pieces of slate, and another flagstone slab for the table. Mortar holds the whole thing together. In order to successfully align the square brass dial with the square slabs that go to make the base and the table, it is necessary, right from start, to orientate the brass slab towards the sun, so that the dial is showing the correct time. Building can then proceed.

CROSS-SECTION OF THE SUNDIAL

Flagstone table
Arranged so the flat face is uppermost

Brass sundial
Aligned with your watch and the sun

Fixing
Plastic wall plugs and rust-proof screws

Broken slate
Set in mortar with joints raked out

Sandstone fragments
Arranged so that the edges and corners are well defined

Mortar infill
Running up the full height of the column

Flagstone slab base

Paving slab

Soil
Compacted

Sand
Raked level

Sundial

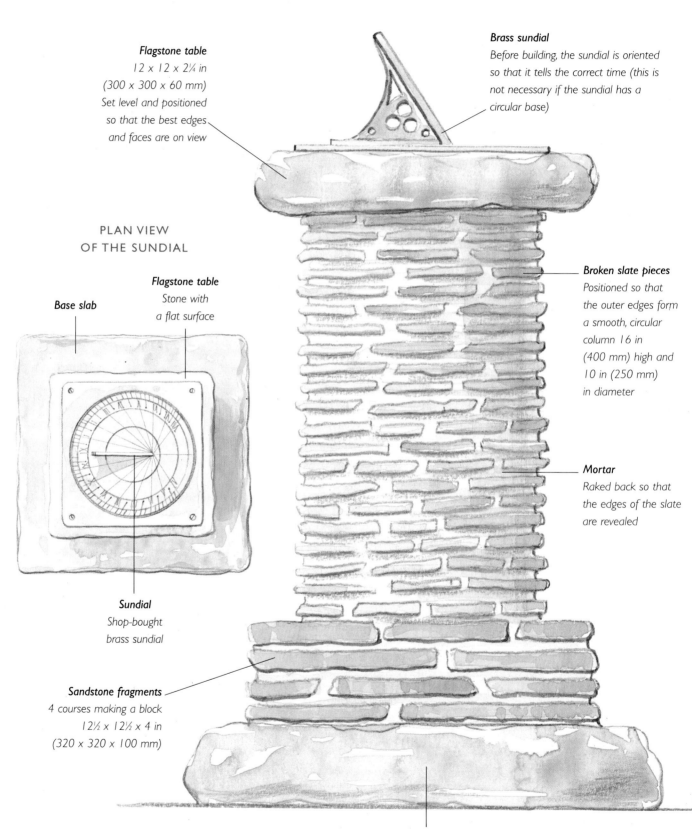

SIDE VIEW OF THE SUNDIAL

Flagstone table
12 x 12 x 2¼ in
(300 x 300 x 60 mm)
Set level and positioned
so that the best edges
and faces are on view

Brass sundial
Before building, the sundial is oriented
so that it tells the correct time (this is
not necessary if the sundial has a
circular base)

**PLAN VIEW
OF THE SUNDIAL**

Base slab

Flagstone table
Stone with
a flat surface

Broken slate pieces
Positioned so that
the outer edges form
a smooth, circular
column 16 in
(400 mm) high and
10 in (250 mm)
in diameter

Mortar
Raked back so that
the edges of the slate
are revealed

Sundial
Shop-bought
brass sundial

Sandstone fragments
4 courses making a block
12½ x 12½ x 4 in
(320 x 320 x 100 mm)

Flagstone base slab
16 x 16 x 3 in (400 x 400 x 80 mm)

EXPLODED VIEW OF THE SUNDIAL

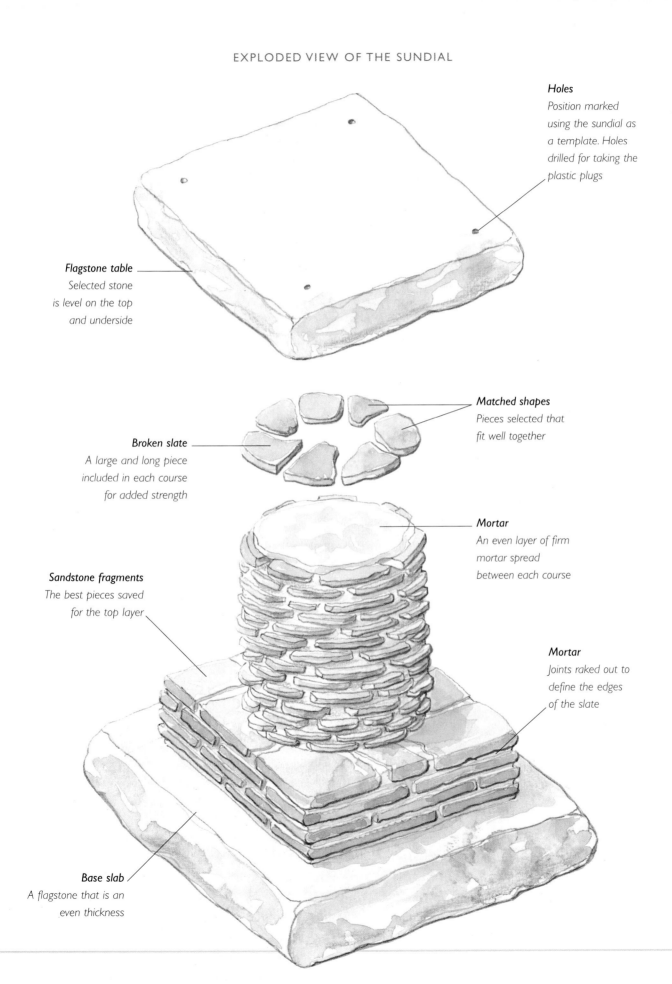

Holes
Position marked using the sundial as a template. Holes drilled for taking the plastic plugs

Flagstone table
Selected stone is level on the top and underside

Matched shapes
Pieces selected that fit well together

Broken slate
A large and long piece included in each course for added strength

Mortar
An even layer of firm mortar spread between each course

Sandstone fragments
The best pieces saved for the top layer

Mortar
Joints raked out to define the edges of the slate

Base slab
A flagstone that is an even thickness

Step-by-step: **Making the sundial**

Alignment
Rotate the base to match the orientation of the sundial

1 Put the brass sundial plate on the ground, check the orientation against the sun and your watch, then set the stone base slab on mortar, aligning it with the brass plate.

Leveling
Use slivers of stone to adjust the level if necessary

Bedding
Bed the slab into the mortar

Trowel work
Tap the stone with the trowel handle until it sits correctly

Mortar
Lay a bed of mortar

Slate circle
Arrange the slate to make a circle 10 in (250 mm) in diameter

Plinth
Build the layers up to a height of 4 in (100 mm)

Bedding
Press the slate into the bed of mortar

2 To build the plinth, use the pointing trowel to butter the base with mortar, and arrange the sandstone to make a 12½ in (320 mm) square. Continue until the plinth is about 4 in (100 mm) high.

3 To build the column, butter mortar on the plinth, and arrange the slate to make a circle 10 in (250 mm) in diameter. Butter the circle with mortar, add another layer of slate, and so on. Check each layer with the tape measure and level.

Circle circumference
*Always aim for a good fit
around the outside edge*

4 Continue laying circles
of slate until the column
is about 16 in (400 mm) high. If
the structure looks as though it
is going to sag, tap stones into
place with the mason's hammer,
and stop to allow the mortar to
stiffen up before continuing.

Adjusting
*Use the mason's
hammer to tap
raised stones
back into line*

Helpful hint

If the day is hot and dry, dip
the slate in water prior to
bedding it in mortar. This
reduces the absorbency of
the stone and prevents it
drawing all the water out of
the mortar. Dip a stone in
water, give it a shake and
then press it in the mortar.

Screwing
*Work carefully to avoid slipping
and damaging the brass*

Alignment
*Double-check the
orientation of the sundial*

Drilling
*Use a masonry
bit to bore holes
in the stone*

Bedding
*Lower the slab
on to the bed
of mortar*

Damping
*Wet the
underside of
the stone to
reduce its
absorbency*

5 Lay the brass plate on the table slab,
and then carefully drill holes, and
plug and screw the plate in position. Be
very careful that you don't over-tighten
the screws and split the stone.

6 Finally, butter the top of the
column with mortar and stand the
slab and sundial in place. Check the
alignment against the sun and your watch.

Flagstone potting table

If you enjoy potting plants, but are fed up with working on that wobbly bench in the greenhouse, or you simply want to build a beautiful potting table in the nineteenth-century English tradition, this project will prove very satisfactory. The table is perfect for displaying plants when not in use for potting.

TIME

Three days (eight hours to lay the foundation slab, fourteen hours to build the two base piers, and a couple of hours to fit the flagstone).

SAFETY

The flagstone slab is extremely heavy – it needs two strong people to lift it into position.

YOU WILL NEED

Materials *for a table 3 ft (1 m) long, 23 in (580 mm) wide, and 32 in (800 mm) high*
- Mortar: 2 parts (66 lb or 30 kg) cement, 1 part (33 lb or 15 kg) lime, 9 parts (300 lb or 135 kg) soft sand
- Concrete: 1 part (94 lb or 50 kg) cement, 2 parts (200 lb or 100 kg) sharp sand, 3 parts (300 lb or 150 kg) aggregate
- Slate or limestone flagstone: 1 flagstone 3 ft (1 m) long, 23 in (580 mm) wide, and 3–3½ in (80–90 mm) thick
- Split limestone: 1 square yard (meter) salvaged roof stone, ½ in (15 mm) thick

- Architectural limestone: 8 salvaged cut and faced stones 10 in (250 mm) long, 6½ in (170 mm) wide, and 5 in (130 mm) thick

Tools
- Tape measure, straight-edge, piece of chalk
- Spade and shovel
- Wheelbarrow and bucket
- Wooden beam: about 24 in (600 mm) long, 3 in (80 mm) wide, and 2 in (50 mm) thick
- Mortar float
- Bricklayer's trowel
- Mason's and drill hammers
- Pointing trowel
- Level

A TABLE FOR ALL SEASONS

This table needs to be built against a strong brick or stone wall in the garden. It could also be sited against a shed. Ideally, you need an area that is tucked away and oriented so that the wall shields you from the wind, while the sun warms your back.

The decorative effect of the piers is achieved by building alternate courses of cut architectural limestone and layered roof stone. The mortar has been raked out in order to create strong shadow lines that draw the eye to the stone. When you are searching out your materials, opt for salvaged stone – choose large blocks showing a dressed face to all sides, and roof stone with cut edges. Spend time in the stoneyard stacking and arranging the various materials available, until you come up with a suitable combination. While all the given measurements are more or less flexible, if you want to vary them, the only proviso is that the pier walls need to be at least 6½ in (170 mm) thick. If, at any point during construction, the walls begin to sag or the mortar oozes from the joints, stop work until the mortar has stiffened up.

CROSS-SECTION OF THE POTTING TABLE

Flagstone table
At least 3 in (80 mm) thick and set with the weathered surface facing uppermost

Split limestone
Salvaged stone known commonly as "roof stone" or "slate stone"

Cut limestone
Arranged so that the freshly cut face is out of sight

Mortar
Raked back to reveal the edge of the stone

Cast concrete foundation

Hardcore
Compacted waste stone

Flagstone potting table

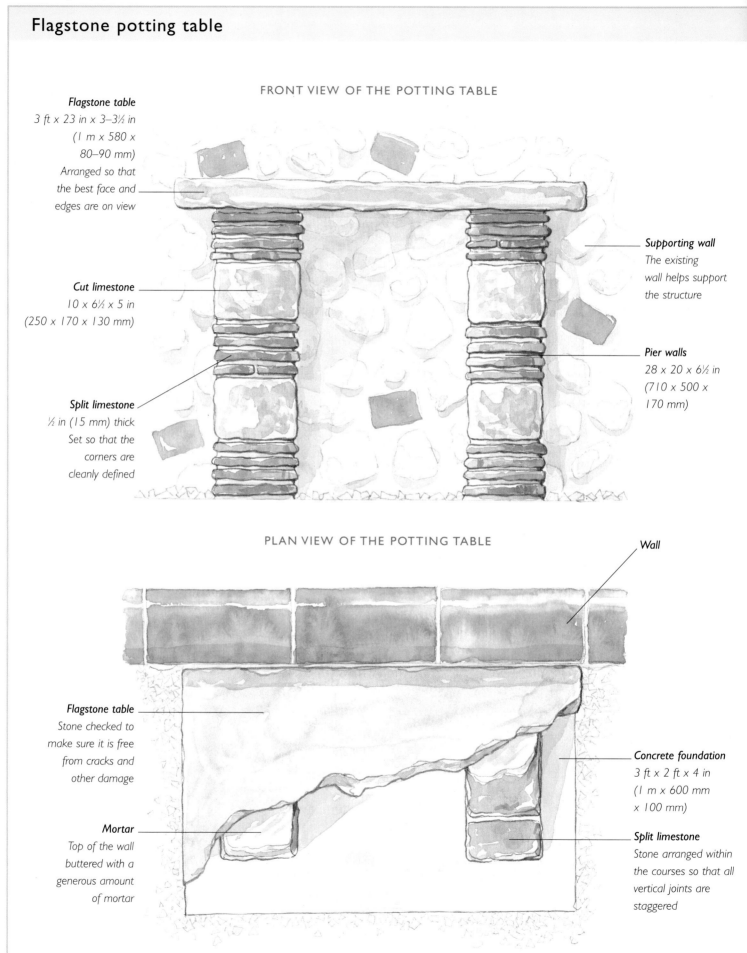

FRONT VIEW OF THE POTTING TABLE

Flagstone table
*3 ft x 23 in x 3–3½ in
(1 m x 580 x
80–90 mm)
Arranged so that
the best face and
edges are on view*

Cut limestone
*10 x 6½ x 5 in
(250 x 170 x 130 mm)*

Split limestone
*½ in (15 mm) thick
Set so that the
corners are
cleanly defined*

Supporting wall
*The existing
wall helps support
the structure*

Pier walls
*28 x 20 x 6½ in
(710 x 500 x
170 mm)*

PLAN VIEW OF THE POTTING TABLE

Wall

Flagstone table
*Stone checked to
make sure it is free
from cracks and
other damage*

Mortar
*Top of the wall
buttered with a
generous amount
of mortar*

Concrete foundation
*3 ft x 2 ft x 4 in
(1 m x 600 mm
x 100 mm)*

Split limestone
*Stone arranged within
the courses so that all
vertical joints are
staggered*

CUT-AWAY VIEW OF THE POTTING TABLE

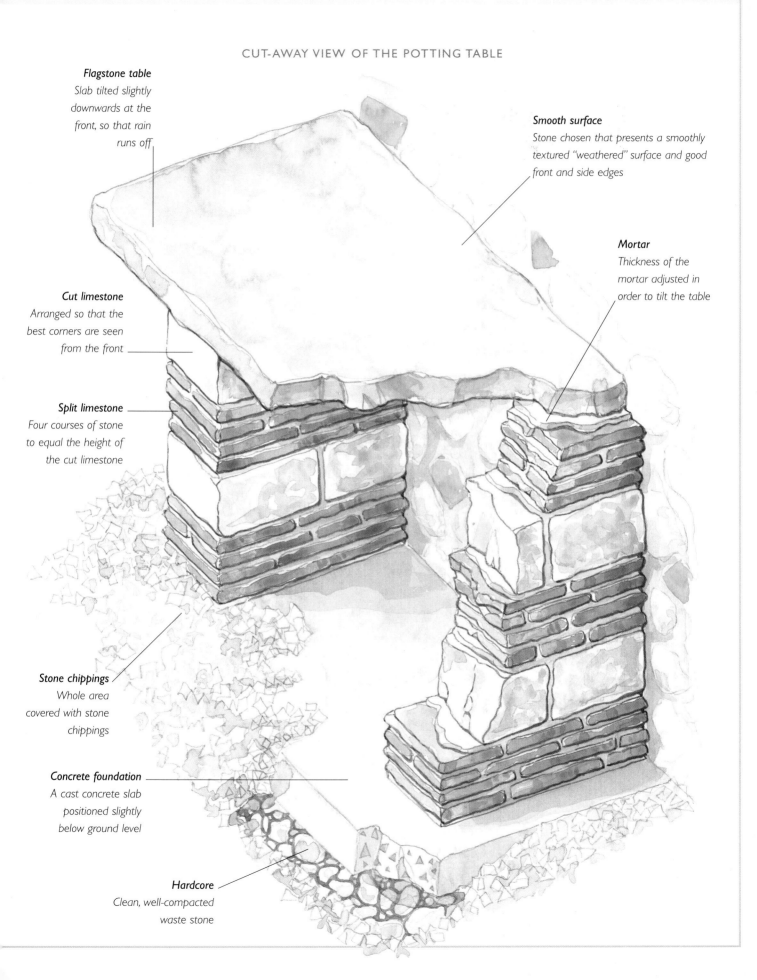

Flagstone table
Slab tilted slightly downwards at the front, so that rain runs off

Smooth surface
Stone chosen that presents a smoothly textured "weathered" surface and good front and side edges

Mortar
Thickness of the mortar adjusted in order to tilt the table

Cut limestone
Arranged so that the best corners are seen from the front

Split limestone
Four courses of stone to equal the height of the cut limestone

Stone chippings
Whole area covered with stone chippings

Concrete foundation
A cast concrete slab positioned slightly below ground level

Hardcore
Clean, well-compacted waste stone

Step-by-step: **Making the flagstone potting table**

Concrete foundation
Aim for a thickness
of 4 in (100 mm)

Piers
Each pier measures 6½ in (170 mm)
thick and 20 in (500 mm) wide

Float
Use the float
to bring the
concrete to a
smooth finish

Guidelines
Use chalk to
mark the
positions of
the piers

Spacing
Set the
piers 16 in
(400 mm)
apart at
the centers

1 Use the spade to clear the foundation area. Make it 3 ft (1 m) wide, 2 ft (600 mm) from front to back, and 8 in (200 mm) deep. Half-fill it with hardcore, then top it off with a layer of concrete 4 in (100 mm) thick. Use the wooden beam and mortar float to bring it to a smooth, level finish.

2 Use the tape measure, chalk and straight-edge to draw out the two piers. They should be 8½ in (215 mm) in from each side of the foundation, and 9 in (230 mm) apart. They measure 6½ in (170 mm) thick, and 20 in (500 mm) deep from front to back.

Wall
The piers must be built
against a wall

Tapping
Tap the
limestone with
the handle of
the trowel to
bed it in the
mortar

3 Butter mortar on the base slab (within the pier markings) with the bricklayer's trowel, and arrange the first course of split limestone. (Trim it to size with the mason's hammer.) Butter the limestone with mortar, and add another layer. Make sure the corners are as crisp as possible. Insert courses of architectural limestone where appropriate, placing the blocks lengthways to run from front to back of the pier. Continue until the courses reach a total height of 28 in (710 mm).

Pier height
The piers are 28 in
(710 mm) high

Height
adjustment
The thin layers
of stone allow
for small
adjustments
in height

Architectural
limestone

4 Use the pointing trowel to rake out some of the mortar from between the various courses. Do it after about every three to four courses.

Pointing
Use the point
of the trowel to
clean out the
courses

Helpful hint

When working on a small project like this, use the large bricklayer's trowel to carry and catch the mortar, and the smaller pointing trowel to do the pointing.

Checking levels
Use the drill
hammer to tap
the slab into
the mortar

5 When you have built both piers, wait until the mortar has begun to set. Then butter the top of the piers with mortar and bed the table slab in place. Check that it is horizontal with the level. If it is not, tap the offending side of the slab with the hammer.

Finishing
Cover the foundation
slab with your
chosen material

Camomile bench

This simple idea is beautifully effective. The stone bench – a bit like a sofa – has the seat planted out with a mixture of grass and camomile. When you sit down on the camomile, its fragrant scent wafts over you. Buy the non-flowering variety of camomile, *Chamaemelum* 'Treneague', which is used to create camomile lawns.

TIME

Two weekends (eight hours to lay the foundation slab, sixteen hours to build the form, and eight hours for planting the camomile and generally tidying up).

SAFETY

The blocks are heavy, so wear gloves and lift them one at a time.

CROSS-SECTION OF THE BENCH

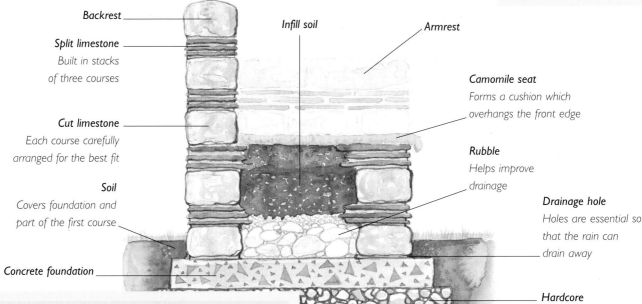

Backrest

Split limestone
Built in stacks of three courses

Cut limestone
Each course carefully arranged for the best fit

Soil
Covers foundation and part of the first course

Concrete foundation

Infill soil

Armrest

Camomile seat
Forms a cushion which overhangs the front edge

Rubble
Helps improve drainage

Drainage hole
Holes are essential so that the rain can drain away

Hardcore
Broken waste stone

YOU WILL NEED

Materials *for a bench 5 ft (1.57 m) long, 29 in (730 mm) wide, and 34 in (870 mm) high*

- Mortar: 2 parts (150 lb or 70 kg) cement, 1 part (75 lb or 35 kg) lime, 9 parts (700 lb or 315 kg) soft sand
- Concrete: 1 part (330 lb or 150 kg) cement, 2 parts (660 lb or 300 kg) sharp sand, 3 parts (1000 lb or 450 kg) aggregate
- Split limestone: 2 square yards (meters) of salvaged roof stone, about ½ in (15 mm) thick
- Architectural limestone: about 60 salvaged cut and faced stones, 10 in (250 mm) long, 6 in (150 mm) wide,

3½–4 in (90–100 mm) thick
- Hardcore: 1 cubic yard (meter)
- Infill topsoil: about 3 wheelbarrow loads

Tools
- Tape measure, straight-edge, piece of chalk
- Casting beams: 2 beams about 5 ft (1.6 m) long, 3 in (80 mm) wide, and 2 in (50 mm) thick
- Wooden tamping beam: 4 ft (1.2 m) long, 3 in (80 mm) wide, and 2 in (50 mm) thick
- Bricklayer's trowel
- Pointing trowel
- Mason's hammer
- Level and wire brush

A COMFORTABLE FRAGRANCE

If you have ever walked barefoot over a camomile lawn and marvelled at its fragrance and the feel of the soft, lush growth, you can imagine that sitting on a cushion of camomile will also be a very pleasant experience. Everything about this project is a joy – the bench makes a very comfortable and exotic seat, the structure is large and decorative enough for even the grandest garden, and the notion of sitting on the camomile is so novel that the bench becomes a great conversation piece. The structure is made up from courses of cut architectural stone alternating with courses of stacked roof stone. The mix of stone gives an interesting finish; the courses of roof stone are also used to level out the inevitable mismatch and stepping that occurs when using salvaged architectural stone. The overall pattern of the coursing is further enhanced by the raked mortar joints.

Camomile bench

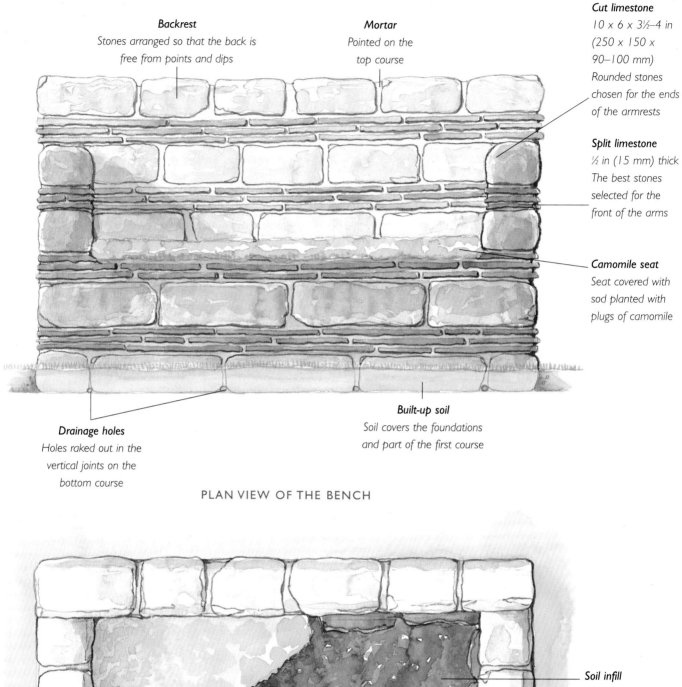

FRONT VIEW OF THE BENCH

Backrest
Stones arranged so that the back is
free from points and dips

Mortar
Pointed on the
top course

Cut limestone
10 x 6 x 3½–4 in
(250 x 150 x
90–100 mm)
Rounded stones
chosen for the ends
of the armrests

Split limestone
½ in (15 mm) thick
The best stones
selected for the
front of the arms

Camomile seat
Seat covered with
sod planted with
plugs of camomile

Drainage holes
Holes raked out in the
vertical joints on the
bottom course

Built-up soil
Soil covers the foundations
and part of the first course

PLAN VIEW OF THE BENCH

Soil infill
Soil allowed to
settle before the
sod and camomile
are planted

Split limestone
Protrudes into the
soil infill

Topsoil
Rich soil that is free
from manure

CUT-AWAY VIEW OF THE BENCH

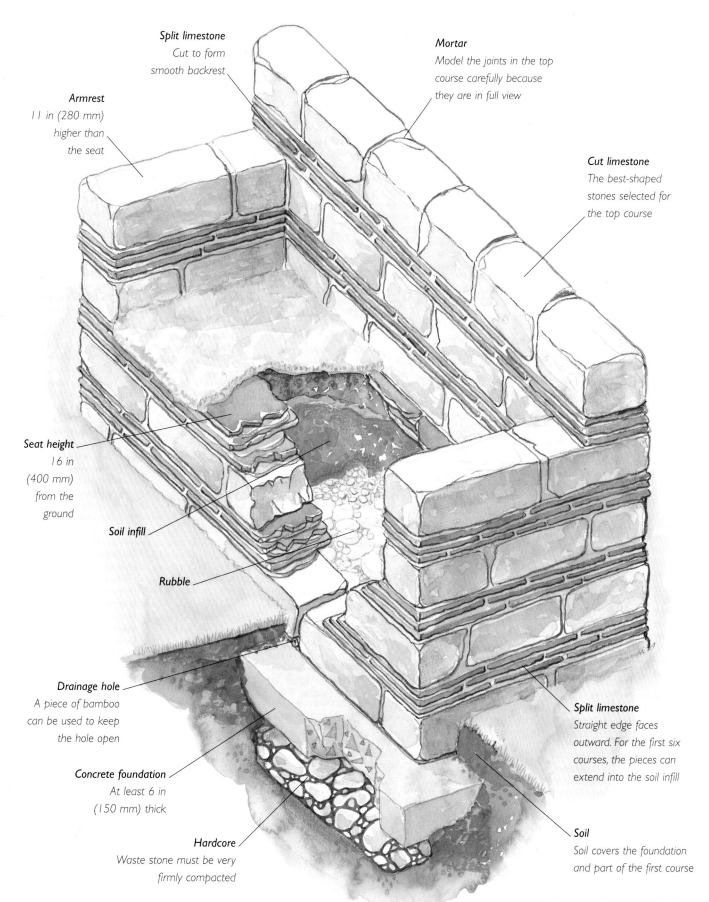

Split limestone
Cut to form
smooth backrest

Mortar
Model the joints in the top
course carefully because
they are in full view

Armrest
11 in (280 mm)
higher than
the seat

Cut limestone
The best-shaped
stones selected for
the top course

Seat height
16 in
(400 mm)
from the
ground

Soil infill

Rubble

Drainage hole
A piece of bamboo
can be used to keep
the hole open

Split limestone
Straight edge faces
outward. For the first six
courses, the pieces can
extend into the soil infill

Concrete foundation
At least 6 in
(150 mm) thick

Hardcore
Waste stone must be very
firmly compacted

Soil
Soil covers the foundation
and part of the first course

Step-by-step: **Making the camomile bench**

Measuring
Use the tape measure to
set out the outline

Foundation
Make the
concrete slab
6 in (150 mm)
thick

Trial fitting
Have a dry fitting
of the stones

Best face
Arrange the
stones so that
the best face
is on view

Best fit
Swap the
stones around
until you have
a well-fitting
arrangement

1 Excavate to a depth of 12 in
(300 mm) and half-fill with
compacted hardcore. Position and level
the casting beams, 3 ft (1 m) apart, and
top them up with concrete. Level with the
tamping beam. Use the tape measure, chalk
and straight-edge to outline the bench
(5 ft x 29 in or 1.57 m x 730 mm).

2 Arrange the blocks of salvaged
architectural stone so that they fit
well and the best cut face is looking to the
chalk line. Wet the blocks and use the
bricklayer's trowel and the pointing trowel
to bed them on stiff mortar.

Infill
Pack the bench with top soil

Leveling
Check each
course using
a level

3 To lay the roof stone,
spread a bed of mortar,
and use the mason's hammer to
carefully trim and arrange the
pieces of stone. Repeat until you
have three courses of roof stone.
Lay a layer of architectural stone.
Continue laying the alternating
courses, and keep checking that
it is all level.

Helpful hint

Spend a lot of time
choosing the roof stone
cornerstones and making
sure they are a good fit, and
the rest of the course will
fall into line more easily.

Cornerstone
Position the architectural cornerstones accurately

Armrest
The armrest course should be tied in with the backrest

4 When you have built up to the level of the seat (about 17 in (430 mm) – two courses of architectural stone and six of roof stone), fill the trough with topsoil, and place the stones for the arms of the seat.

Armrest height
Build up to a height of 11 in (280 mm) above the seat level

Backrest
Build the back using three courses of roof stone and one course of cut limestone

5 Build the arms to 11 in (280 mm) above the level of the seat (two courses of architectural stone and three of roof stone). Continue building the back to a total height of 34 in (870 mm) above the ground.

Cleaning
Make a special job of cleaning the top of the backrest

6 Finally, when the mortar is well cured, use a wire brush to clean all faces of the structure. Be careful not to blur the crisp finish of the mortar.

Cleaning
Make sure that you clean the mortar from the faces of the cut stone

Wire brushing
Use the brush to define the courses and generally clean up the stonework

Pedestal table

One of the joys of having a garden is being able to sit outside on a summer's evening and slowly sip a long, cool drink, relaxing in a comfortable chair. The picture is completed by the unique pedestal table that holds your drink.

TIME

Two weekends (eight hours to lay the foundation slab, eighteen hours to build the column, and a couple of hours to fit the flagstone).

SAFETY

The flagstone slab is incredibly heavy – it needs at least four strong, fit people to lift it.

YOU WILL NEED

Materials *for a table 36 in (900 mm) square and 36 in (900 mm) high*

- Mortar: 2 parts (175 lb or 80 kg) cement, 1 part (90 lb or 40 kg) lime, 9 parts (800 lb or 360 kg) soft sand
- Concrete: 1 part (94 lb or 50 kg) cement, 2 parts (200 lb or 100 kg) sharp sand, 3 parts (300 lb or 150 kg) aggregate
- Slate or limestone flagstone for the table: about 3 ft (900 mm) square and 5 in (130 mm) thick
- Flagstones for the plinth and capital: 2 stones about 22 in (570 mm) square and 3½ in (90 mm) thick
- Split limestone: 1 cubic yard (meter) of salvaged roof stone, ½ in (15 mm) thick

- Hardcore: 0.5 cubic yards (meters) of broken stone

Tools

- Wheelbarrow and bucket
- Hand truck
- Tape measure, straight-edge, piece of chalk
- Spade and shovel
- Sledgehammer
- Sawn wood: 4 lengths, about 26 in (660 mm) long, 3 in (80 mm) wide, and 2 in (50 mm) thick
- Wooden beam: about 24 in (600 mm) long, 3 in (80 mm) wide, and 2 in (50 mm) thick
- Mortar float
- Level
- String and peg
- Bricklayer's trowel
- Mason's hammer
- Pointing trowel

ALL AROUND THE TABLE

In the context of this book, this project is monolithic. There is about one cubic yard (meter) of roof stone in the column, and the slab that goes to make the tabletop is so heavy that it takes four strong people to lift it into position. So you must start by assessing how you are going to shift the stone. For example, if you want the table at the end of the garden – over a bridge, the other side of the pond, and behind the border – it presents quite a challenge. You will have to ask family and neighbours to help. We used a wheelbarrow for the roof stone, and a hand truck for the slabs.

The procedure for building the column is to select and shape pieces of roof stone to fit the circumference of the circle, set them in mortar, fill in the circle with more pieces of slate, and then move on to the next layer of mortar. Every few courses, rake out the mortar to reveal the slate, and make checks with the level to ensure that the stones remain true.

CROSS-SECTION OF THE TABLE

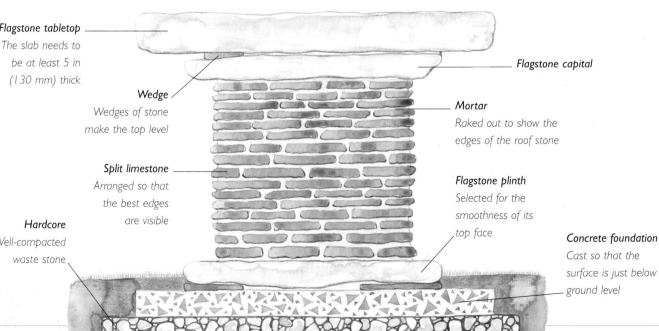

Flagstone tabletop
The slab needs to be at least 5 in (130 mm) thick

Flagstone capital

Wedge
Wedges of stone make the top level

Mortar
Raked out to show the edges of the roof stone

Split limestone
Arranged so that the best edges are visible

Flagstone plinth
Selected for the smoothness of its top face

Hardcore
Well-compacted waste stone

Concrete foundation
Cast so that the surface is just below ground level

Pedestal table

FRONT VIEW OF THE TABLE

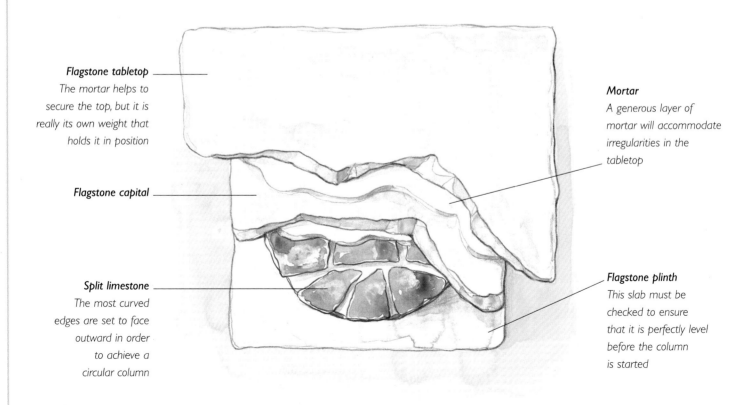

Flagstone tabletop
*3 ft x 3 ft x 5 in
(900 x 900 x 130 mm)
Slab set on a
thick bed of mortar*

Wedge
*If necessary, a wedge
is tapped between
the slabs to stabilize
the tabletop*

Mortar
*Mortar allowed to
stiffen after every
three or four courses*

Flagstone capital
*22 x 22 x 3½ in
(570 x 570 x 90 mm)
Edges that slope back from top
to bottom improve the design*

Split limestone
*½ in (15 mm) thick (if split
limestone is not available, old
roofing tiles could be substituted)*

Flagstone plinth
*22 x 22 x 3½ in
(570 x 570 x 90 mm)
Even though this stone is not
in full view, it does need to be
level on the top face and have
good edges*

PLAN VIEW OF THE TABLE

Flagstone tabletop
*The mortar helps to
secure the top, but it is
really its own weight that
holds it in position*

Flagstone capital

Split limestone
*The most curved
edges are set to face
outward in order
to achieve a
circular column*

Mortar
*A generous layer of
mortar will accommodate
irregularities in the
tabletop*

Flagstone plinth
*This slab must be
checked to ensure
that it is perfectly level
before the column
is started*

EXPLODED VIEW OF THE TABLE

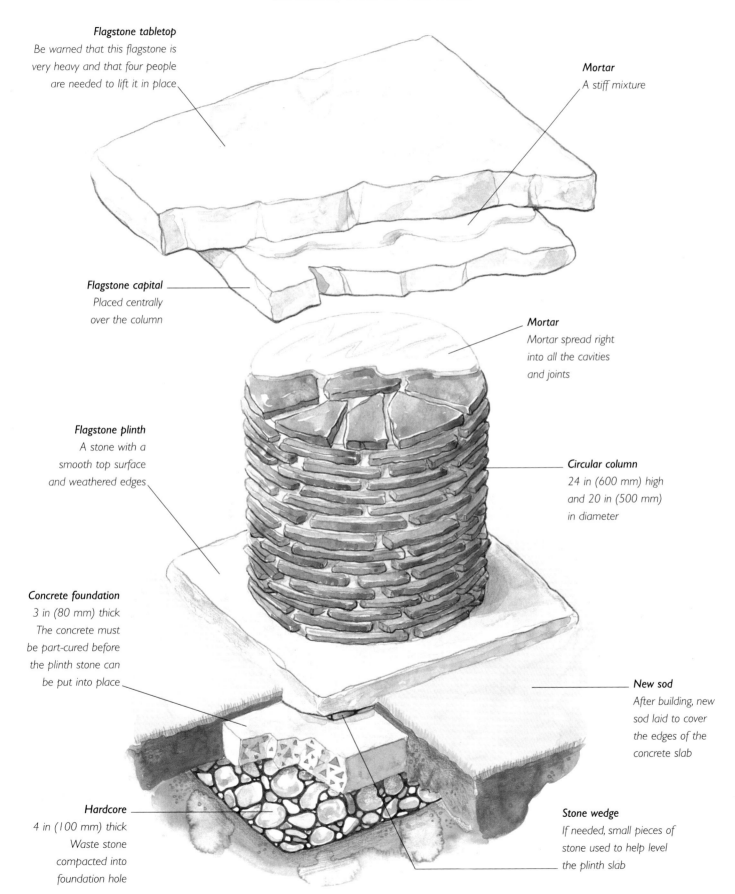

Flagstone tabletop
Be warned that this flagstone is very heavy and that four people are needed to lift it in place

Mortar
A stiff mixture

Flagstone capital
Placed centrally over the column

Mortar
Mortar spread right into all the cavities and joints

Flagstone plinth
A stone with a smooth top surface and weathered edges

Circular column
24 in (600 mm) high and 20 in (500 mm) in diameter

Concrete foundation
3 in (80 mm) thick
The concrete must be part-cured before the plinth stone can be put into place

New sod
After building, new sod laid to cover the edges of the concrete slab

Hardcore
4 in (100 mm) thick
Waste stone compacted into foundation hole

Stone wedge
If needed, small pieces of stone used to help level the plinth slab

Step-by-step: Making the pedestal table

Floating
Float the concrete to a smooth finish

Split limestone
Pile up the stone so that it is close at hand

Frame
The frame measures 25 in (640 mm) square

Leveling
Use the level to check that the slab is horizontal

Alignment
Position the plinth stone by using the chalked diagonals

1 Dig out the foundation to a depth of about 8 in (200 mm), making it 25 in (640 mm) square, and half-fill it with hardcore. Ram it down with the sledgehammer. With the lengths of sawn wood, build a rough frame on the hardcore, measuring 25 in (640 mm) square and 3 in (80 mm) deep. Fill it up with concrete, and smooth it off with the wooden beam and mortar float.

2 When the concrete has set, remove the frame. Draw diagonals across the base slab to establish the center, then set the plinth stone in place. Check that it is level. If it is not, insert slivers of stone until it lies horizontal.

Circle of stone
Bed the split stone in mortar to make a 20 in (500 mm)-diameter circle

Leveling
Check the level after every five courses

Pointing
Pack the mortar under the edges of the plinth stone

Hammering
Tap individual stones to achieve an overall level surface

Trimming
Trim the edges of the stone for the best fit

3 Draw diagonals to establish the center of the plinth stone, then draw a circle 20 in (500 mm) in diameter using the string and peg. Use the bricklayer's trowel to butter the circle with mortar and place split limestone around the edge.

4 Build up about five layers of limestone, then go round with the mason's hammer tapping individual stones into line. Make repeated checks with the level. Continue building until the column is 24 in (600 mm) high.

Adjusting
Tap raised stones
back into line

Bedding
Butter the top of the column
with a generous layer of mortar

Filling
Fill the
cavities with
mortar and
stone waste

Coursing
Rake out
the mortar to
reveal the
edges of
the stone

Column height
Aim for
a height
of 24 in
(600 mm)

5 Walk around the column, checking that the sides are vertical, and use the mason's hammer to tap stones that are raised back into line.

6 Use the pointing trowel to butter the top of the finished column with a generous layer of mortar and carefully set the capital stone in place. Make sure that it is aligned with the plinth stone.

Mortar bedding
Butter the top of the capital
slab with a thick bed of mortar

7 Butter the capital slab with a thick layer of mortar, and then call on your helpers to lift the table slab into place. Check that it is level. If necessary, put slices of waste stone underneath to adjust the level until it lies horizontal.

Wedging
Use slices of
waste stone
underneath the
slab to maintain
the level

Helpful hint

If you intend doing heavy stonework – moving slabs or bags of cement, or even if you want to take some of the effort out of gardening, a traditional hand truck is ideal.

Glossary

Backfilling To fill a hole around a foundation or wall with earth.

Bedding The process of pressing a stone into a bed or layer of wet mortar and ensuring that it is level.

Buttering The act of using a trowel to cover a piece of stone with wet mortar just prior to setting it in place on the bed of mortar.

Cobbles Smooth, rounded stones.

Compacting Using a hammer or the weight of your body to press down a layer of sand, earth or hardcore.

Course A term describing the horizontal lines or layers of stone that make a wall or structure.

Coursing A general term describing the process of bedding a number of stones in mortar in order to build a course.

Curing time The time taken for mortar or concrete to become firm and stable. Part-cured mortar or concrete is firm enough to take a small amount of weight.

Damping Wetting the stone just prior to bedding in on mortar.

Dressing The act of using a hammer, chisel or trowel to trim a stone to a level, smooth, or textured finish.

Dry run See Trial run.

Floating The procedure of using a metal, plastic or wooden float to skim wet concrete or mortar to a smooth and completely level finish.

Hardcore Pieces of stone, brick, or concrete in a range of sizes that will pack together to form a firm base or foundation.

Leveling Using a level to decide whether or not a structure or stone is level, and then making adjustments to bring individual stones into line.

Marking out Using a string, pegs and tape measure to set out the size of a foundation on the ground, also to mark out an individual stone in readiness for cutting to size.

Pointing Using a trowel, stick, or an alternative tool of your choice to bring the mortar joints to the desired finish.

Raking out Using a trowel to rake out part of the mortar, so that the edges of the stone are clearly revealed.

Sighting To judge by eye, or to look down or along a wall in order to determine whether or not the structure is level.

Siting Deciding whereabouts on the site – in the garden or on the plot – the structure is going to be placed.

Tamping The act of using a length of wood to compact and level wet concrete.

Tessellated tile Tile or pavers in geometric shapes that fit together to form patterns. As used in this book, pavers larger than typical mosaic tile.

Trial run Running through a procedure of setting out a structure without using concrete or mortar, in order to ascertain whether or not the envisaged project or technique is feasible.

Trimming Using a hammer, chisel or the edge of large trowel to bring the edge of a piece of stone to a good finish.

Wedging Using small slivers of stone to bring larger pieces up to the desired level.

Wire brushing The act of using a wire brush to remove dry mortar from the face of the stone.

Conversion chart

To convert metric measurements to English measurements, simply multiply the figure given in the text by the relevant number shown in the table below. Bear in mind that conversions will not necessarily work out exactly, and you will need to round the figure up or down slightly. (Do not use a combination of metric and English measurements – for accuracy, keep to one system.)

To convert	Multiply by
millimeters to inches	0.0394
meters to feet	3.28
meters to yards	1.093
sq millimeters to sq inches	0.00155
sq meters to sq feet	10.76
sq meters to sq yards	1.195
cu meters to cu feet	35.31
cu meters to cu yards	1.308
grams to pounds	0.0022
kilograms to pounds	2.2046
liters to gallons	0.22

Index

Acknowledgments

The authors are grateful to Ian Parsons (photographer) for helping to lift the heaviest stones.

AG&G Books would like to thank the following picture libraries for their contribution: *Dennis Davis Photography Design* (pages 68, 94 top and 94 bottom); *Garden and Wildlife Matters* (pages 46 bottom and 69 inset) and *John Glover Photography* (page 46 top).

Reading List

Other Storey Titles you will enjoy:

Building Stone Walls, by John Vivian. Includes equipment requirements, instructions for creating wall foundations, information on coping with drainage problems, and hints for incorporating gates, fences, and stiles. 122 pages. Paperback. ISBN 0-88266-074-8.

Building with Stone, by Charles McRaven. An introduction to the art and craft of creating stone structures with step-by-step project instructions. 192 pages. Paperback. ISBN 0-88266-550-2.

Build Your Own Stone House Using the Easy Slipform Method, by Karl and Susan Schwenke. Complete instructions on tools, materials, estimating, siting, excavating, and using and removing forms. 176 pages. Paperback. ISBN 0-88266-639-8.

Natural Stonescapes: The Art and Craft of Stone Placement, by Richard L. Dubé and Frederick C. Campbell. With this start-to-finish guide, anyone can design and build stone groupings modeled after geological formations found in nature with professional results. Practical tips for choosing stones and more than 20 sample designs are included. 176 pages. Paperback. ISBN 1-58017-092-7.

Outdoor Water Features: 16 Easy-to-Build Projects for Your Yard and Garden, by Alan and Gill Bridgewater. Clear step-by-step photographs and instructions make it easy to create attractive water features in your own back yard. Choose among a classic wall-mounted fountain spout, a traditional cascade and garden pond, a Japanese-style bamboo water pump, witty water sculptures, and more! 128 pages. Paperback. ISBN 0-58017-334-9.

Step-by-Step Outdoor Stonework: Over Twenty Easy-to-Build Projects for Your Patio and Garden, edited by Mike Lawrence. From walls, arches, patios, paths, steps, rock gardens, and fountains to seats, tables, sundials, and bird baths, this book is the definitive guide to working with stone in your garden. 96 pages. Paperback. ISBN 0-88266-891-9.

Stonescaping: A Guide to Using Stone in Your Garden, by Jan Kowalczewski Whitner. Learn to incorporate stone into many garden features, including steps, walls, paths, ponds, and rock gardens. Features 20 basic designs. 168 pages. Paperback. ISBN 0-88266-755-6.

Stonework: Techniques and Projects, by Charles McRaven. Learn to collect and handle stone while creating walls, stairs, pools, and even waterfalls! 192 pages. Paperback. ISBN 0-88266-976-1.

These books and other Storey Books are available at your bookstore, farm store, garden center, or directly from Storey Books, Schoolhouse Road, Pownal, Vermont 05261, or by calling 1-800-441-5700. Or visit our Web site at www.storeybooks.com